EARNINGS PER SHARE
AND MANAGEMENT DECISIONS

EARNINGS PER SHARE
AND MANAGEMENT DECISIONS

John F. Childs

Prentice-Hall, Inc.   Englewood Cliffs, N. J.

PRENTICE-HALL INTERNATIONAL, INC., *London*
PRENTICE-HALL OF AUSTRALIA, PTY. LTD., *Sydney*
PRENTICE-HALL OF CANADA, LTD., *Toronto*
PRENTICE-HALL OF INDIA PRIVATE LTD., *New Delhi*
PRENTICE-HALL OF JAPAN, INC., *Tokyo*

Library of Congress
Catalog Card Number: 76-135758

Second Printing.....January, 1972

Printed in the United States of America
ISBN-0-13-222521-2
B & P

My first two books were dedicated to my daughter, Susan, and I also dedicate this one to her. I am pleased that she did the illustrations in this book.

ABOUT THE AUTHOR

John F. Childs is an advisor, lecturer and writer on all phases of corporate finance. His two major books on finance *Long-Term Financing* (1961) and *Profit Goals and Capital Management* (1968) were published by Prentice-Hall, Inc. The latter is a more detailed study of some of the material covered in this book.

Mr. Childs has worked in Wall Street for over 30 years and is now a senior officer of a major New York bank. He is a Director of the American Management Association, the Atomic Industrial Forum and the Florida Power Corporation. He has degrees from Trinity College, Harvard Business School, and Fordham Law School, and is a member of the New York Bar.

ACKNOWLEDGEMENTS

Presumably most authors are like this author who finds it hard to stand criticism of his "baby." However, the author wishes to acknowledge the kind and unkind criticisms that were made by his associates—Anthony H. Meyer, T. Carter Hagaman and Brian J. Heidtke—during revision after revision. No matter how much some of their criticisms hurt, they were an invaluable help.

TABLE OF CONTENTS

TABLES

10

EARNINGS PER SHARE
AND MANAGEMENT DECISIONS

AUTHOR'S INTRODUCTION

WHAT WE WILL COVER

Earnings per share are stockholders' primary interest. They have to be because the two benefits a stockholder receives—dividends and market appreciation—both come from earnings per share. Because of stockholder interest, management must be deeply concerned with earnings per share. Since the stockholders are the owners of the business, management should not differentiate between what is good for a company and what is good for its stockholders.

However, we raise the question whether management can produce the proper results for its stockholders if it uses increasing earnings per share, particularly current earnings per share, as a guide for capital and financial decisions. Answering this question will be the primary concern of this book.

In the Introduction, we will define three financial terms and look briefly at how management may view earnings per share. So armed, we will consider the causes of changes in earnings per share in Chapter One. At that point, we will not answer the question of whether increasing current earnings per share is a good management guide. We will first suggest, in Chapter Two, a better guide—Profit Goals—based on Cost-of-Capital. With that background we will show in Chapter Three why increasing current earnings per share is a poor guide. In Chapter Four, we will show how venture capital companies play the earnings per share game and grow to success or failure. In Chapter Five, we will back track and relate profits to the stockholder's return. And because earnings per share are so important to stockholders, we will say a few words about management's attitude towards earnings and market price in the concluding Chapter Six.

This is a short book and, therefore, will omit much detail. Our purpose is to paint with a broad brush, illustrating some basic principles which may point the direction in which management may wish to do more thinking. And these ideas may also be of interest to investors who wish to judge management's performance.

DEFINITION OF TERMS

We will take the next few pages to define what we mean by returns on capital, long term capital and common equity. This is essential to understanding the book.

RETURNS ON CAPITAL

Returns on capital are important for this book because we will utilize them in explaining increases in earnings per share. Furthermore, we will explain how management should think of returns on capital in making capital decisions.

We will use two returns: Return on Common Book Value (Common Equity) and Return on Long Term Capital After Taxes. Their components are shown in Table I.

VALIDITY OF EARNINGS

These returns will have significance only if they are analyzed in terms of all the circumstances surrounding a company.

The validity of reported earnings will have an important bearing on the returns. Are earnings over or understated because of such factors as non-recurring income or expense, the accounting treatment of depreciation, juggling of advertising or research and development expenditures, etc.?

The type of business in which a company is engaged and the nature of its assets will have to be kept in mind. For example, if a company has a large amount of cash being held temporarily for

Table I

CAPITAL AND RETURNS ON CAPITAL COMPONENTS

Figures from Consolidated Balance Sheet and Income Statement

$$\underline{\text{RETURN ON COMMON BOOK VALUE}} = \frac{\text{NET INCOME AVAILABLE FOR COMMON EQUITY AFTER INTEREST, TAXES AND PREFERRED DIVIDENDS}}{\text{COMMON BOOK VALUE}}$$

COMMON BOOK VALUE (COMMON EQUITY)

	Balance Sheet	Income Statement
Common par or stated value	$	NET INCOME AVAILABLE
Capital surplus	$	FOR COMMON EQUITY
Earned surplus (retained earnings)	$	AFTER INTEREST, TAXES AND
Common Book Value (Common Equity)	$	PREFERRED DIVIDENDS $

$$\underline{\text{RETURN ON LONG TERM CAPITAL AFTER TAXES}} = \frac{\text{RETURN}}{\text{LONG TERM CAPITAL}}$$

LONG TERM CAPITAL   RETURN

	Balance Sheet		Income Statement	
			Interest component on	
Finance leases capitalized	$		finance lease payments	$
Mortgage bonds	$		Interest	$
Debentures	$		Interest	$
Short term debt				
continuously renewed	$		Interest	$
Convertible debentures	$		Interest	$
Income bonds	$		Interest	$
Long Term debt		$	Total Interest	$
Preferred	$		Dividends	$
Convertible preferred	$		Dividends	$
Total preferred		$	Total preferred dividends	$
			Total charges on	
Total Senior securities		$	senior securities	$
Minority interest		$	Income applicable to minority interest	$
			Net income available	
Common equity (common book value)		$	for common equity	$
Long Term Capital		$	Return	$

capital investment, the returns on capital might be understandably low because of the lack of earnings on the cash.

LONG TERM CAPITAL

Capital is important; it represents investment and investors must be compensated. We refer to the liability side of the balance sheet and use long term capital as our measure. And from our point of view, it ties in with our financial thinking. Management may prefer to use a different base for measuring performance, such as total assets, plant plus working capital, or even sales. However, the measurement standard employed must be consistent with the return on long term capital objective.

Long term capital includes long term debt (that is, debt with a maturity longer than one year), preferred stock, convertibles and common equity. Without going into detail, we might note that non-seasonal current bank loans and commercial paper with a maturity of less than one year, which are continuously renewed, are in fact long term debt. They provide long term capital as a result of their renewal. Leases of a financial nature are comparable to long term debt. They should be capitalized and included in long term debt.

Long term capital can be very complicated if it includes numerous layers of different types of securities of a parent company and subsidiaries. In order to simplify the picture, we will talk primarily about two broad types of securities—long term debt and common equity. When we speak of any part of long term capital, such as debt, representing a certain percentage, we mean that part as a percent of long term capital.

COMMON EQUITY (COMMON BOOK VALUE)

Perhaps the most important part of long term capital with which we are concerned is the book value of the common equity. Common equity includes the par or stated value of the common stock, capital surplus and earned surplus. It represents proceeds from the sale of stock and earnings retained after dividends. We will use the term common book value as meaning the same as common equity. Common book value per share is merely the total common equity divided by the number of shares of common stock outstanding.

SIGNIFICANCE OF BOOK FIGURES

The significance of common book value, of course, depends on the valuation of the company's assets. If the assets are overvalued then the book value does not represent sound value. On the other hand, the assets may be undervalued and consequently the book value will understate the stockholders' true net equity on the assets. A natural resource company may have valuable assets not fully reflected on its books. A company may have valuable patents which are not recorded on its books. When interpreting return on capital, it would be preferable to have the assets restated on the basis of today's value and the common book value adjusted accordingly. For some companies this would show a substantially different picture from the reported balance sheet. Management should be aware of this difference and visualize the effect of the difference in its interpretation of ratios based on such figures.[1]

Common book value may be overstated if a company has a large amount of convertible preferred stock which appears on the balance sheet at a low nominal value, but which has a dividend rate justifying a higher value. Then, liquidating value may be more representative and the common stock should be reduced accordingly. Such a situation may arise when a company acquires another company with convertible preferred.[2] For this reason, some of the common equities of conglomerates are grossly overstated.

We cannot avoid commenting on the knotty question of how to treat reserve accounts of various types. Only those reserves which represent common equity (on an after tax basis) should be included in long term capital. All other reserves should be left out, recognizing

---

[1] In the long run, a company should make an adequate return on these adjusted measures of capital. In viewing a company's past results, the returns on capital should include an allowance for the benefits of the increased asset value.

[2] Company A issues 100,000 shares of 6% convertible preferred with a market value of $100 per share, a liquidating value of $100 per share, and a total market value of $10,000,000 to acquire company B's common stock which has a total market value of $10,000,000 but which has a book value of $5,000,000. In a pooling of interests, company A may record the convertible preferred stock on its books at the book value of the stock acquired which is $5,000,000 or $50 per share. (Actually, Company A can record the preferred at any value it wishes.) The convertible preferred with a liquidating value and a market value of $100 per share really should be recorded on the company's books at approximately $100 per share to show correctly the claims prior to the common in the capital structure. This would require a corresponding reduction in common equity. Opinion No. 10 of the Accounting Principles Board recommends that the liquidation preference of the stock be disclosed in the equity section of the balance sheet in the aggregate, either parenthetically, or in short.

all the while that their presence may affect the overall profit potential or risk characteristics of the company. For a more detailed discussion of the treatment of reserves see Appendix A.

Thus, while we fully recognize the many deficiencies of reported long term capital and common book value as measures of capital, we do need bases on which to measure returns and they will serve the purpose in our discussion of the significance of earnings per share. There are some people who pooh pooh book value and returns of capital as having no significance. In doing so, they overlook the importance of capital as a base on which to measure profits in a competitive economic system.

HOW MANAGEMENT MAY VIEW EARNINGS PER SHARE

Before we discuss how earnings per share grow, let's consider how management may look at earnings per share and why.

Management reports to its stockholders at least annually on the progress of earnings per share; this tends to make management focus

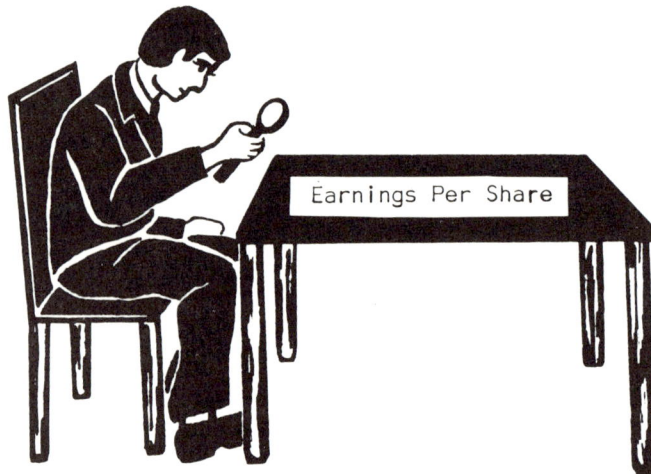

MANAGEMENT MAY TAKE A SHORT RANGE VIEW OF EARNINGS PER SHARE.

on current earnings. Financial analysts are sensitive to latest reported earnings and, today, particularly, they seem to be oriented towards short range gains. Some analysts tend to project future prospects for earnings based on past and most current earnings and they pressure management unduly to show immediate gains in earnings per share. They may be highly critical of management which issues new common stock, thereby causing a dilution in current earnings per share. Some investment bankers, desiring to obtain underwriting business and, consequently, trying to please management, bias their financing advice towards what will have the most immediate favorable impact on earnings per share.

And there are some managements who are short range stock market minded almost to the point of manipulation. They may be anxious, for selfish reasons, to take advantage of short term expediencies during a prosperous period. Their careers in top management may be limited to relatively few years. They may wish to be acclaimed as dynamic in business magazines. They may attempt to make a financial killing through stock options or stock purchases. Managements of companies which are subject to a take-over may be impelled to do almost anything to boost current earnings per share and the price-earnings ratio in order to save their skins.

Thus management is influenced, pressured and may have personal reasons to view earnings per share with a magnifying glass rather than a telescope.

John F. Childs

ONE

HOW EARNINGS PER SHARE GROW

If some managements view earnings per share as we have implied that they do, will they make correct capital and financial decisions? In order to answer this question we will examine in this chapter how earnings per share grow.

A well informed management should know the causes of changes in earnings per share and the extent to which each of the various causes contributes to the total change in a company's earnings per share. We question whether some managements have taken the time to separate out the various causes. In case you feel that managements have done so, you might try asking a top management group for an answer to the following simple question:

> What will be the compound growth rate in earnings per share for a company—earning, and continuing to earn, 10% on its common book value and paying out 50% of its earnings in dividends?

You may be surprised by many of the replies. Actually, dividend payout policy is one of the basic causes of changes in earnings per share.

We will concentrate on increases; decreases generally result from reverse circumstances. We will discuss:

  I. Plow back of earnings
 II. Sale of common stock above book value
III. High price-earnings ratio company acquiring a low price-earnings ratio company in a stock swap.
IV. Increase in rate of return on common book value
  V.   Leverage
VI. Retirement of common stock

I. PLOW BACK OF EARNINGS

A company seldom pays out all of its earnings in dividends. Retained or "plowed back" earnings provide more capital for the company to invest. If the company continues to earn the same rate on its old investment and earns anything at all on the new investment, earnings per share will increase. The simple formula for the growth rate in earnings per share from plow back is:

The percent earned on common book value multiplied by the percent of earnings retained, provided the rate of return on common book value and the dividend payout ratio remain steady.

The percent of earnings retained is merely 100% of the total earnings less the percent paid out.

This is illustrated in Table II for a company with a return of 10% on common book value and a dividend payout ratio of 50%. The formula would be: 10% earned on common book value multiplied by 50% of earnings retained, giving a 5% compound growth rate in earnings, dividends and common book value per share.

Examples of compound growth rates with various constant rates of return and payouts are shown in Table III.

The simple formula can be adopted to the case when the rate on the old investment remains constant and the return on the new investment is constant but they are different in amount. The effect of compounding through plow back in such a situation can be calculated by using the rate of earnings on the new capital provided by the retained earnings because compounding from plow back depends on the earnings on the new investment. This is illustrated in Table IV.

If there is a change in the return on the old investment, the simple formula cannot be used to determine the growth rate from plow back. Such a change will in itself have an effect on the result.

The last comments may appear to over-complicate the idea of plow back. The point to keep in mind is that earnings per share increase due to the earnings on the added investment and, with a steady return and dividend payout, the growth rate can readily be determined.

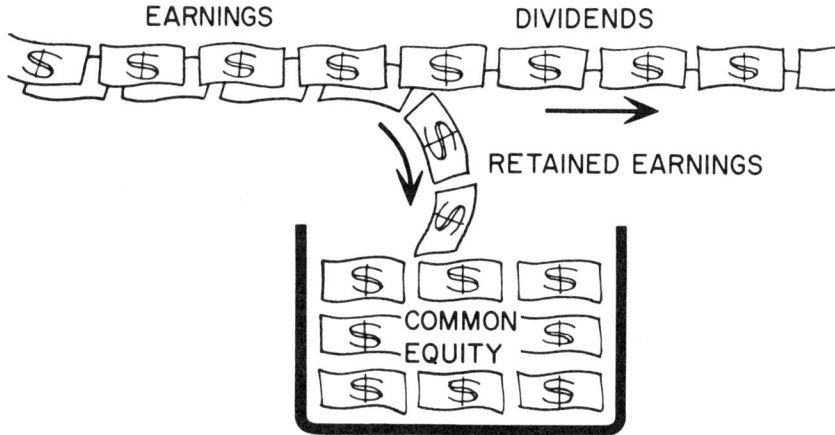

EARNINGS   DIVIDENDS

RETAINED EARNINGS

COMMON EQUITY

PLOW BACK BUILDS THE BASE FOR INCREASING EARNINGS PER SHARE.

Table II

INCREASE IN EARNINGS PER SHARE FROM PLOW BACK

Part 1

10% RETURN ON COMMON BOOK VALUE AND 50% DIVIDEND PAYOUT PRODUCES A 5% GROWTH RATE IN EARNINGS PER SHARE

Line		Year 1	Year 2	Year 3
1	Common Book Value Per Share	$100.00	$105.00	$110.25
2	% Return on Common Book Value	10%	Same	Same
3	Earnings Per Share	$ 10.00	$ 10.50	$ 11.025
4	% Earnings Paid out in Dividends	50%	Same	Same
5	Dividends per Share	$ 5.00	$ 5.25	$ 5.5125
6	Retained Earnings per Share	$ 5.00	$ 5.25	$ 5.5125
7	Growth Rate in Earnings Per Share from:			
	Plow Back		5%	5%

Part 2

EFFECT OF PLOW BACK ON BALANCE SHEET AND INCOME STATEMENT

Line		Year 1	Year 2	Year 3
	BALANCE SHEET			
1	Assets	$175.00	$184.00	$193.00

LIABILITIES

2	Liabilities	$ 75.00	$ 79.00	$ 82.75
3	Common Equity—1 share	$100.00	$105.00	$110.25
4	Total	$175.00	$184.00	$193.00

INCOME STATEMENT

5	Sales	$200.00	$210.00	$220.5000
6	Expenses, taxes and interest	$190.00	$199.50	$209.4750
7	Net Income. (Earnings Per Share)	$ 10.00	$ 10.50	$ 11.0250
8	Dividends (Payout ratio 50%)	$ 5.00	$ 5.25	$ 5.5125
9	To Retained Earnings	$ 5.00	$ 5.25	$ 5.5125

Table III

SOME COMPOUND GROWTH RATES IN
EARNINGS PER SHARE FROM PLOW BACK
WITH CONSTANT RATE OF RETURN AND PAYOUT

Column Line	I Return on Common Book Value	II Dividend Payout Ratio	III Compound Growth Rate in Earnings Per Share
1	10%	25%	7.50%
2	15	,,	11.25
3	20	,,	15.00
4	10	50%	5.00%
5	15	,,	7.50
6	20	,,	10.00
7	10	65%	3.50%
8	15	,,	5.25
9	20	,,	7.00

Table IV

GROWTH RATE IN EARNINGS PER SHARE FROM PLOW BACK WHEN RETURN ON OLD INVESTMENT AND NEW INVESTMENT ARE CONSTANT BUT DIFFERENT IN AMOUNT, WITH CONSTANT DIVIDEND PAYOUT RATIO

Return on Old Common Book Value 20%, Return on New Common Book
Value 10% and Dividend Payout Ratio 50%
Return on New Common Book Value 10% x 50% of Earnings Retained =
5% Growth Rate in Earnings per Share
All Funds Generated in One Year Are Reinvested at the Beginning
of the Next Year

Line		Year 1	Year 2	Year 3	Year 4
	OLD INVESTMENT				
1	Common book value per share	$100	Same	Same	Same
2	Return	20%	,,	,,	,,
3	Earnings per share	$ 20	,,	,,	,,
4	Dividend payout ratio	50%	,,	,,	,,
5	Dividend	$ 10	,,	,,	,,
6	Retained earnings	$ 10	,,	,,	,,
7	Earned surplus		$10.00	$20.00	$30.00
	NEW INVESTMENT				
	Earned surplus				
8	From above		$10.00	$20.00	$30.000
9	From new investment			$ 0.50	$ 1.525
10	Total		$10.00	$20.50	$31.525
11	Return		10%	Same	Same
12	Earnings per share		$ 1.00	$ 2.05	$ 3.1525
13	Dividend payout ratio		50%	Same	Same
14	Dividend		$ 0.50	$ 1.025	$ 1.5763
15	Retained earnings		$ 0.50	$ 1.025	$ 1.5763
	OLD AND NEW INVESTMENT				
16	Earnings per share	$ 20	$21.00	$22.05	$23.1525
17	GROWTH RATE IN EARNINGS PER SHARE		5%	5%	5%

Plow back of earnings, with a stable return on common book
value, is the only sure way to have continous growth in earnings per
share.

Managements have a tendency to speak with pride about any increase in earnings per share. It should be expected that as a result of the additional capital from retained earnings, earnings per share will increase. There is something wrong if they don't!

Some managements, desiring to show growth in earnings per share, pounce on the idea of having a low dividend payout ratio in order to increase the effect of plow back. Dividend policy is not that simple. We do not wish to interrupt our discussion to cover dividend policy. However, in order to avoid leaving the impression that a low dividend payout is necessarily a good way to increase earnings per share, we have included a brief discussion of dividend policy in Appendix B.

Now that we have finished our explanation of plow back, we will only raise the question whether an increase in earnings per share from plow back means that management has made correct decisions on investing retained earnings—the answer later.

II. SALE OF COMMON STOCK ABOVE BOOK VALUE

If a company sells new stock, there will be an immediate reduction in earnings per share because of the greater number of shares outstanding, assuming no immediate earnings on the new money raised by the offering. Generally, in a common stock financing, an offering of 10% new common is a reasonable size; this means one new share for each ten existing shares. It will reduce earnings per share immediately by 9.09% as shown in Table V, Part 1. This is what management fears about an offering of common stock.

However, temporary dilution does not tell all the story. In the first place, the full impact of the reduction in earnings per share can be cushioned if the company invests the proceeds in temporary investments to provide some income. But more important, it is possible that after the money is put to work in a capital investment the earnings per share will increase. Whether they do or not depends on two factors: One, the net proceeds per share the company receives from the sale of the new stock compared to the existing common book value per share; two, the rate earned on the new investment compared with the rate earned on the existing investment.

If stock is sold above book value and the same rate is earned on the new investment as on the existing common book value, earnings per share will increase as a result of the sale of common.

Table V

EFFECT OF SALE OF STOCK ON EARNINGS PER SHARE

Part 1

IMMEDIATE REDUCTION IN EARNINGS PER SHARE FROM SALE OF COMMON STOCK ABOVE BOOK VALUE

1 for 10 Offering

Column	I	II	III
	Outstanding	New Stock	Total
Line			
1 Number of Common Shares	10	1	11
Common Book Value			
2 Total	$1,000	$120*	$1,120
3 Per Share	$ 100		$ 101.82
4 Return on Common Book Value	10%		
Earnings for Common			
5 Total	$ 100	0	$ 100
6 Per Share	$ 10	0	$ 9.09
7 Price-earnings ratio	13		
8 Market Price	$ 130		
9 Decrease in earnings per share			-9.09%

Part 2

ULTIMATE INCREASE IN EARNINGS PER SHARE FROM SALE OF STOCK ABOVE BOOK VALUE
1 for 10 Offering

Column	I	II	III
	Outstanding	New Stock	Total
Line			
1 Number of Common Shares	10	1	11
Common Book Value			
2 Total	$1,000	$120*	$1,120
3 Per Share	$ 100		$ 101.82
4 Return on Common Book Value	10%	10%	10%
Earnings for Common			
5 Total	$ 100	$ 12	$ 112
6 Per Share	$ 10		$ 10.182
7 Increase in earnings per share			+1.82%
8 Price-earnings ratio	13		13
9 Market price	$ 130		$ 132.37

*Net proceeds per share received by the company is $120 compared with a market price of $130. The difference makes allowance for financing expenses, etc.

This is illustrated in Table V, Part 2. We have assumed in the table that the stock is selling for $130 at a price-earnings ratio of 13 times. We have further assumed that the net proceeds received by the company from the sale of stock, after allowing for financing costs, is $120 compared with a book value of $100.

Earnings per share increase from $10.00 per share to $10.182, or 1.82% through the sale of stock after the company puts the money to work and earns 10% on it after taxes. With the same price-earnings ratio, the market price for the stock also increases. Thus the sale of stock may increase earnings per share after the capital has been put to work and may not be as painful as it is made out to be.[1] Since most companies do not sell stock often, we would

[1] If the financing had been done with debt, assuming a 6% interest rate and 50% tax rate, earnings per share would have shown a smaller immediate reduction to $9.64 or 3.6%, and when the funds were put to work at 10%, a greater increase to $10.84 or 8.4%.

not expect a very large increase in earnings per share from this source.

Of course, some combination of net proceeds per share received for new stock and the rate earned on the investment of the proceeds can result in a decrease in earnings per share. For example, if the net proceeds per share for the new stock equalled the existing common book value per share and the return on the new investment were below the return on the old investment; earnings per share would decrease. And even if the net proceeds per share for the new stock were above the existing common book value, earnings per share could decrease if the return on the new investment were sufficiently below the return on the old investment.

Even if earnings increase through the sale of common, we again raise the question without answering it—has capital been properly used and is the earnings increase enough?

III. HIGH PRICE-EARNINGS RATIO COMPANY ACQUIRING A LOW PRICE-EARNINGS RATIO COMPANY IN A STOCK SWAP

If the price-earnings ratio of the stock of the acquiring company is higher than the price per share paid to the seller, divided by the seller's earnings per share, and the acquisition is accounted for on a pooling of interests basis, the current earnings per share of the acquiring company will be increased.

To put it another way, if the earnings-price percentage of the acquiring company is lower than the earnings-price percentage paid for the acquired company, the acquiring company will increase its current earnings per share. This is illustrated in Table VI, which can be summarized as follows:

1. Company A and Company B have the same $10 earnings per share but Company A has more glamour and sells for 20 times earnings whereas Company B sells for 15 times.
2. The exchange ratio is based on market prices of $200 for Company A and $150 for Company B so that Company A issues 3/4 of a share for one share of Company B.

3.   The combined companies have total earnings of $20 and earnings per share of $11.429 ($20 total earnings ÷ 1 3/4 shares).
4.   The dividend payout ratios for both companies are 100% so that there will be no increase in earnings per share from plow back.
5.   In year 1, Company A's earnings per share increase from $10.00 to $11.429 due to the acquisition. There is no further increase in year 2.
6.   Therefore, growth in earnings per share of Company A goes from 0% in year 1 before the acquisition to 14.29% after, and back to 0% in the second year.

The size of the acquisition, as well as the difference in the price-earnings ratios, will have an important bearing on the extent to which Company A's earnings per share are affected. In Table VI, the acquired Company B was as large as Company A, and therefore, the resulting increase was large.

In the table, both companies have the same return on common book value before the acquisition so that there was no change after. This, of course, would not necessarily occur. Which company had the higher return, the acquiring company or the one being acquired, would determine whether the acquisition would result in an increase in return on common book value. It would also be affected by the value at which the acquired company is recorded.

The important point to note in Table VI is that the growth in earnings per share is a one shot proposition. Growth from this source goes from 0% to 14.29% and back to 0%.

If both companies had a dividend payout ratio of 50%, then their growth rates from plow back, prior to acquisition, would be 5%. This results from the 10% return on common book value multiplied by the 50% of earnings retained. Then, in the year of the acquisition the increase in earnings per share from the acquisition of 14.29% would be added to the growth rate from plow back of 5% making a total of 19.29%. The year after the acquisition the growth rate would fall back to 5%.

The large jump in earnings per share from an acquisition may excite unsuspecting investors and the stock price may react accord-

Table VI

INCREASE IN EARNINGS PER SHARE FROM HIGH PRICE-EARNINGS RATIO COMPANY ACQUIRING A LOW PRICE-EARNINGS RATIO COMPANY IN A STOCK SWAP

Based on Market Prices, Company A Issues 3/4 of a Share
Of Its Stock for 1 share of Company B.
Acquisition Accomplished on First Day of Year—Assumes Complete
Pooling of Interests

Column	I	II	III	IV
	Company A	Company B	Company A + Company B	Company A + Company B
	Year 1	Year 1	Year 1	Year 2
Line				
1 Number of shares common	1	1	1 3/4	1 3/4
Common book value				
2 Total	$100	$100	$200	$200
3 Per share	$100	$100	$114.29	$114.29
4 Return on common book value	10%	10%	10%	10%
Earnings for Common				
5 Total	$ 10	$ 10	$ 20	$ 20
6 Per share	$ 10	$ 10	$ 11.429	$ 11.429
7 Dividend payout ratio	100%	100%	100%	100%
8 Dividends per share	$ 10	$ 10	$ 11.429	$ 11.429
9 Retained earnings per share	0	0	0	0
10 Price-earnings ratio	20	15	17 1/2	17 1/2
11 Market price	$200	$150	$200	$200
Growth Rate in earnings per share from:				
12 Plow back	0	0	0	0
13 Acquisition			14.29%	0
14 Total			14.29%	

ACQUISITION--SINGLE SHOT EFFECT ON EARNINGS PER SHARE.

ingly.[2] However, to sustain this rate of growth the company will have to make additional acquisitions in even greater size or volume.

In Table VI, we assumed that the price-earnings ratio would settle down between the price-earnings ratio of the two companies so that the market price of Company A's stock would continue to sell for $200. During the conglomerate fever, before the stock market decline in 1969, more than likely the price-earnings ratio of Company A would have increased after the acquisition. The subsequent market fate of a number of the conglomerates shows that such high price-earnings ratios are not sustainable.

Growth in earnings per share can be generated either internally or externally. Management should not intimate that external growth from acquisitions can be sustained. Much doubt should be cast upon a management that talks about its external growth in earnings per share through acquisitions.

The Accounting Principles Board of the American Institute of Certified Public Accountants finally issued a watered down opinion in 1970 permitting pooling where the security used is common stock. Thus for all practical purposes the door has been left wide open to use this approach to jazz up earnings per share.

At this point, we leave this cause of increasing earings per share by merely challenging your thinking as to whether external growth in earnings per share is a good acquisition guide.

---

[2]In reporting most recent comparative earnings, accountants require companies to show most recent earnings compared with the previous year, with the acquired company included in the previous year. However, "as reported" figures can also be shown. Furthermore, previous years' earnings are often not restated in the ten year summary in the back of many annual reports. As a consequence, the growth rate in earnings per share may mislead investors.

IV. INCREASE IN RATE OF RETURN ON COMMON BOOK VALUE

Earnings per share will increase if there is an increase in the rate of return on common book value.

In fact, generally, a change in the rate of return on existing common book value is translated directly into an equal increase or decrease in earnings per share. This is shown in Table VII. To make it simple, sales and profits are shown as increasing without any increase in assets on the assumption that the assets had not been fully utilized. All earnings are paid out in dividends so that there is no increase from plow back of earnings.

Table VII

INCREASE IN EARNINGS PER SHARE FROM INCREASE IN RATE OF RETURN ON COMMON BOOK VALUE

Line		Year 1	Year 2	Year 3
	BALANCE SHEET			
1	Assets	$175.00	$175.00	$175.00
	Liabilities			
2	Liabilities	75.00	75.00	75.00
3	Common Equity–1 share	100.00	100.00	100.00
4	Total	$175.00	$175.00	$175.00
	INCOME STATEMENT			
5	Sales	$200.00	$210.00	$220.500
6	Expenses, taxes and interest	190.00	199.50	209.475
7	Net Income (Earnings per share)	$ 10.00 →$ 10.50 →	$ 11.025	
8	Dividends (Payout ratio 100%)	10.00	10.50	11.025
9	Retained earnings	$ 0.00	$ 0.00	$ 0.000
10	Return on Common Book Value	10.00% →10.50% →	11.025%	
11	Increase in Return on Common Book Value		5.0 %	5.0 %
	Growth Rate in Earnings Per Share from:			
12	Plow back		0.0 %	0.0 %
13	Increase in Return on Common Book Value		5.0 %	5.0 %

There are many ways in which the return on common book value can be increased such as:

1. An increase in return on assets from their more profitable use.
2. A decrease in charges on senior securities from refunding or retirement.
3. Leverage.

If a company has been a poor earner in the past, it may be easier to increase the return on common book value, say from 5% to 10% over a number of years (a 100% increase), than to continue to increase it to 15% (only a 50% increase). Competition tends to exert pressure to hold down the rate of return a company can earn. Similarly, a new company with no earnings may find it easier to show dramatic increases in return on common book value and earnings per share in its early life than later on as it matures and its earnings rate has attained a higher level.

In planning for the future and in estimating the possibilities of future earnings per share, management should distinguish between increases from plow back and increases from a higher rate of return on common. It also should recognize the added difficulty in increasing rate of return as it climbs into the higher levels.

Is an increase in earnings per share due to an increase in return on common book value a sign that management has used capital wisely? An answer later.

V. LEVERAGE

Leverage is the use of senior capital which carries a fixed cost. If the company can earn more on this capital than its fixed cost, the excess earnings will increase the earnings available for the common stock. Increasing the proportion of senior capital is one way to increase earnings per share for the common.

Leverage can be produced by any type of senior security. Preferred stock provides leverage for common. Debt securities have a double barrelled effect because interest charges reduce taxes while preferred dividends are an after tax charge.

Table VIII

NO CHANGE IN EARNINGS PER SHARE WITH NO CHANGE IN LEVERAGE
Same 10% Return on Long Term Capital *After* Taxes

Column	I		II		III
			NO CHANGE IN LEVERAGE		Percent
Line	Amount	Percent	Amount	Percent	Change
1. Debt	$ 20		$ 20		
2. New Debt	____		3		
3. Total Debt	$ 20	20%	$ 23	20%	0%
4. Common Equity – 4 shares	80		80		
5. New Common Equity* – 0.6 shares			12		
6. Total Common Equity	$ 80	80%	$ 92	80%	
7. Long Term Capital	$100	100%	$115	100%	
8. Income before taxes and interest	$ 18.80		$ 21.62		
9. Taxes, assuming 50% rate[†]	8.80		10.12		
10. Income after taxes before Interest	$ 10.00		$ 11.50		
11. Less: Interest on debt 6%	1.20		1.20		
12. Interest on new debt 6%‡	____		0.18		
13. Net Income for Common	$ 8.80		$ 10.12		
14. Return on Long Term Capital *before* taxes	18.80% —— Same ——→ 18.80%				
15. Return on Long Term Capital *after* taxes	10.00% —— Same ——→ 10.00%				0%
16. Return on Common Book Value	11.00% —— Same ——→ 11.00%				0%
17. Earnings per share	$ 2.20 —— Same ——→ $ 2.20				0%

*New common stock is assumed to be sold so as to produce net proceeds per share equal to the existing book value per share.

[†] Line 8 less lines 11 and 12 times 50%.

‡ The interest rate is kept the same on new debt as on existing debt because the risk for the debt holder is the same with the same proportion of debt and the same earnings rate.

We will illustrate leverage with three tables using debt as the senior security. The first table will show what happens when there is no increase in leverage. The second table will show how the earnings for the common will increase with leverage with no increase in the *after* tax return on long term capital. The third table will show the full effect of debt leverage, including the effect of larger interest charges in reducing the effect of taxes. We will now describe each of these tables.

In Table VIII there is no change in leverage. New capital amounting to $15 is added with debt and common equity kept in the same proportion as existed previously. With the return on long term capital after taxes remaining the same, there is no change in the return on common book value or earnings per share. And also there is no change in the return on long term capital *before* taxes.

In Table IX, there is an increase in leverage with the entire new capital of $15 added to debt. In this table, we are only concerned with what happens *after* taxes. The return on long term capital *after* taxes is the same—10% in both columns I and II, while the debt ratio is increased from 20% to 30%. As a result, the return on common book value and earnings per share are both increased 5%. The figures from Table IX are summarized as follows:

Column	I	II	III
			Percent Change
Debt as a percent of long term capital	20%	30%	+50%
Return on long term capital *after* taxes	10%	10%	0%
Return on common book value	11%	11.56%	+ 5%
Earnings per share	$2.20	$2.31	+ 5%

We should note in this table that with increased leverage, less return on long term capital *before* taxes was needed to provide the same return *after* taxes, because of the overall tax savings due to the larger interest charges.

In Table X, we start with the return *before* taxes and increase debt to the same extent as in the previous table. In line 8 of the table the return on long term capital *before* taxes is the same 18.80% in

Table IX

INCREASE IN EARNINGS PER SHARE WITH INCREASE IN LEVERAGE
Same 10% Return on Long Term Capital After Taxes

Column		I		II INCREASE IN LEVERAGE		III
Line		Amount	Percent	Amount	Percent	Percent Change
1.	Debt	$ 20		$ 20		
2.	New debt			15		
3.	Total debt	$ 20	20%	$ 35	30%	+50%
4.	Common equity–4 shares	80		80		
5.	New Common Equity			0		
6.	Total Common Equity	$80	80%	$ 80	70%	
7.	Long Term Capital	$100	100%	$115	100%	
8.	Income before taxes and Interest	$ 18.80		$ 20.75		
9.	Taxes, assuming 50% rate*	8.80		9.25		
10.	Income after taxes before Interest	$ 10.00		$ 11.50		
11.	Less: Interest on debt–6%	1.20		1.20		
12.	Interest on new debt –7%†			1.05		
13.	Net income for common	$ 8.80		$ 9.25		
14.	Return on Long Term Capital *before* taxes	18.80% ⟶ 18.04%				-4%
15.	Return on Long Term Capital *after* taxes	10.00% — Same ⟶ 10.00%				0%
16.	Return on Common Book Value	11.00% ⟶ 11.56%				+5%
17.	Earnings per share	$ 2.20 ⟶ $ 2.31				+5%

*Line 8 less line 11 and 12 times 50%

†Interest rate is increased, because the risk for the debt holder is increased with the greater proportion of debt.

both columns I and II. As a result of the larger interest charges, the effect of taxes is reduced, and, as shown in line 15, there is an increase in return on long term capital *after* taxes from 10.00% to 10.38%, a 3.8% increase. In line 16, the return on common book

Table X
INCREASE IN EARNINGS PER SHARE WITH INCREASE IN LEVERAGE
AND THE TAX SAVINGS EFFECT ON INTEREST

Same 18.80% Return on Long Term Capital *Before* Taxes

Column	I		II		III
			INCREASE IN LEVERAGE		
Line	Amount	Percent	Amount	Percent	Percent Change
1. Debt	$ 20		$ 20		
2. New Debt			15		
3. Total Debt	$ 20	20%	$ 35	30%	+50%
4. Common Equity—4 shares	80	80	80		
5. New Common Equity			0		
6. Total Common Equity	$ 80	80%	$80	70%	
7. Long Term Capital	$100	100%	$115	100%	
8. Income Before Taxes and Before Interest	$ 18.80		$ 21.62		
9. Taxes, assuming 50% rate*	8.80		9.69		
10. Income after taxes before Interest	$ 10.00		$ 11.94		
11. Less: Interest on Debt—6%	1.20		1.20		
12. Interest on New Debt—7%†			1.05		
13. Net Income for Common	$ 8.80		$9.69		
14. Return on Long Term Capital *before* Taxes	18.80% — Same → 18.80%				0%
15. Return on Long Term Capital *after* Taxes	10.00%		→ 10.38%		+3.8%
16. Return on Common Book Value	11.00%		→ 12.11%		+10%
17. Earnings Per Share	$ 2.20		→ $ 2.42		+10%

*Line 8 less line 11 and 12 times 50%.

†Interest rate is increased, because the risk for the debt holder is increased with the greater proportion of debt.

value increases from 11.0% to 12.11%, a 10% increase. And in the last line earnings per share increase from $2.20 to $2.42, also a 10% increase.

The figures from Table X are summarized as follows:

Column	I	II	III
			Percent Change
Debt as a percent of long term capital	20%	30%	+50%
Return on long term capital *before* taxes	18.80%	18.80%	0%
Return on long term capital *after* taxes	10.00%	10.38%	+3.8%
Return on common book value	11.00%	12.11%	+10.0%
Earnings per share	$2.20	$2.42	+10.0%

Since leverage increases earnings per share and return on common book value, the extent of the leverage must be kept in mind when viewing an increase in these two figures. Preferably, when viewing a company's earning performance, returns on capital should be used which eliminate leverage. We have a choice between a *before* tax and *after* return on long term capital.

As shown above, the *before* tax return eliminates the entire effect of leverage.

The *after* tax return on long term capital eliminates part of the effect of leverage, but not the effect of the overall tax reduction because of the interest charges. In spite of this deficiency, we generally prefer the *after* tax return because it is directly comparable with the return required by investors and ties in with our Cost-of-Capital calculation which we will discuss subsequently.

With the dramatic possibility of increasing earnings per share from leverage, why shouldn't management use leverage to the greatest extent possible? In other words, why shouldn't a company borrow at all times the maximum it can borrow? Isn't this an excellent and easy way to increase earnings per share? While we will not interrupt our discussion of earnings per share to answer this question, we will state our opinion: The use of senior securities to the extent that undue financial risk is not added to a company is the proper use of leverage; it benefits the common stockholders. However, we feel strongly that the use of an excessive amount of senior securities will work to the stockholders' detriment in the long run.

Because it is so easy to fall into the trap of excessive leverage we have included some remarks on capital structure in Appendix C.

But we have to ask the question whether increases in earnings per share are sufficient justification for a company to sell bonds with 4% net interest cost after taxes and invest the money in a project earning 6% after taxes? Again no answer at this point.

LEVERAGE PAST A CERTAIN POINT IS WORSE THAN TRYING TO PICK YOURSELF UP BY THE BOOT STRAPS—IT MAY BE A COMPANY'S UNDOING.

VI. RETIREMENT OF COMMON STOCK

Retirement of common stock reduces the number of shares outstanding and generally increases earnings per share.

The proceeds used to retire the common can come from cash, sale of an asset, or sale of a senior security. If cash is used, there will be an increase in earnings per share if the company is showing any earnings. When funds are obtained through the sale of assets or a senior security, earnings per share will increase if the after tax return on assets sold, or the after tax carrying cost for the senior security, is less than the earnings-price percentage at which the stock is retired. Thus, one of the factors affecting earnings per share is the source of funds. It also depends on the price at which the stock is retired in relation to the earnings.

The figures in Table XI illustrate the effect of the source of funds. The figures in Part I, with the common retired with cash, show an increase in earnings per share from $5.00 to $5.56.

In Part 2 of Table XI, after retiring common through the sale of the temporary investments, earnings per share increased from $5.00 to $5.33. There would be no change in current earnings per share if the price-earnings ratio were 50 times and the reciprocal, the earnings-price percentage, were 2%. If the price-earnings ratio were higher or the earnings-price percentage lower, there would be a decrease in current earnings.

In Part 3 of Table XI, where the common is retired with debt, earnings per share increased from $5.00 to $5.22. The break even point in this case is a price-earnings ratio of 33 1/3 times or an earnings-price percentage of 3%.

Table XI

INCREASE IN EARNINGS PER SHARE FROM RETIREMENT OF COMMON STOCK

ASSUMED DATA

Line
1. Total Income for Common Equity | $ 5,000,000
2. Shares Outstanding | 1,000,000
3. Earnings Per Share | $5
4. Market Price | $100
5. Price-Earnings Ratio | 20
6. Earnings-Price Ratio | 5%
7. Funds Required to Retire Shares | $10,000,000
8. Shares Retired ($10,000,000 ÷ $100) | 100,000
9. Shares Remaining Outstanding | 900,000
10. Corporate Tax Rate | 50%

Part 1

RETIREMENT WITH CASH

11.	Total Income for Common Equity	$ 5,000,000
12.	Income Lost	0
13.	Remaining Income	$ 5,000,000
14.	Earnings Per Share ($5,000,000 ÷ 900,000)	$5.56

Part 2

RETIREMENT WITH PROCEEDS FROM THE SALE OF ASSETS CONSISTING
OF U.S. TREASURY BILLS YIELDING 4% OR 2% AFTER 50% TAX

15.	Total Income for Common Equity	$ 5,000,000
16.	Income Lost, after tax ($10,000,000 x 2%)	200,000
17.	Remaining Income	$ 4,800,000
18.	Earnings Per Share ($4,800,000 ÷ 900,000)	$5.33

Part 3

RETIREMENT WITH THE PROCEEDS FROM THE SALE OF LONG TERM
DEBT AT 6% INTEREST, OR 3% AFTER 50% TAX

19.	Total Income for Common Equity	$ 5,000,000
20.	Additional expenses, after tax ($10,000,000 x 3%)	300,000
21.	Remaining Income	$ 4,700,000
22.	Earnings Per Share ($4,700,000 ÷ 900,000)	$5.22

It may be noted that the percent increase in earnings per share from retirement of common stock will generally not be the same as the percent change in the rate of return on common book value.

Purchase of a company's own stock may be analyzed like an investment, but can management use an increase in earnings per share as a guide for decision making for this "investment"? Are there not many other factors that have to be weighed such as the purpose, the effect on the debt ratio and the purchase price? If you are interested in the other factors, we have included a brief discussion in Appendix D.

COMBINATION OF CAUSES OF EARNINGS CHANGE

Now let's put together the combined effect of two of the principal causes of growth in earnings per share: plow back and increase in return on common book value. An illustration of the combined effect is shown in Table XII.

In year 1, there is a 5% increase in earnings per share from plow back as a result of a 10% return on common book value and a 50% payout ratio.

In year 2, there is a 5% increase in earnings per share because

Table XII

INCREASE AND DECREASE IN EARNINGS PER SHARE FROM PLOW BACK AND CHANGE IN RETURN ON COMMON BOOK VALUE AND PYRAMIDING EFFECT ON MARKET PRICE THROUGH CHANGE IN PRICE-EARNINGS RATIO

All new Funds Generated in One Year are Reinvested at the Beginning of the Next Year

Line		Year 1	Year 2	Year 3	Year 4	Year 5
1	Common Book Value per share	$100.00	$105.00	$110.51	$116.31	$123.71
2	% return on common book value	10%	10.5%	10.5%	12%	11%
3	Earnings per share	$ 10.00	$ 11.03	$ 11.60	$ 13.96	$ 13.61
4	Dividend payout ratio	50%	50%	50%	47%	48%
5	Dividends per share	$ 5.00	$ 5.51	$ 5.80	$ 6.56	$ 6.53
6	Retained earnings per share	$ 5.00	$ 5.51	$ 5.80	$ 7.40	$ 7.08
7	Price-earnings ratio	10	15	12	20	11
8	Market price	$100	$165	$139	$279	$150
	Growth rate in earnings per share from:					
9	Plow back	5.0%	5.3%	5.3%	6.4%	5.7%
10	Change in return on common book value		5.0%	0.0	14.2	-8.3
11	Total		10.3%	5.3%	20.6%	-2.6%

the return on common book value increases from 10.0% to 10.5%. This increase is not repetitive like plow back. There is also a 5.3% (rounded from 5.25%) increase in earnings per share from plow back as a result of the 10.5% return on common book value and 50% payout ratio. Thus in year 2, there is a total increase in earnings per share of 10.3%—5% from an increase in return on common book value and 5.3% from plow back.

In year 3, if the return on common book value stopped growing as shown in the table, the growth rate would depend on plow back alone and settle back to 5.3% as a result of a 10.5% return on common book value and a 50% payout ratio.

In year 4, we show a further increase in return on common book value to 12% and then in year 5 a decrease to 11%. These changes, along with plow back assuming no increase in dividends, cause wide percentage changes in earnings per share.

The point which is apparent here is that a change in the rate of return on common book value will generally have a greater immediate impact than plow back, assuming no change in dividend payout ratio. However, unlike earnings growth from plowback, which continues year after year, earnings growth from a rising rate of return continues only so long as rate of return continues to rise.

The average year to year growth rate in earnings per share for the four years was 8.4%. However, if we take a broad view of the figures, we note that the average return on common book value was about 11%. If the company anticipates that this is representative of what it may earn in the future, then with a dividend payout ratio of 50% the long range growth rate in earnings per share would depend on plow back and be about 5 1/2%.

We have also included in the table the market prices resulting from these earnings, based on assumed price-earnings ratios. Obviously, changes in earnings per share as well as the price-earnings ratios can result in substantial swings in market price.

REVIEW OF CAUSES OF EARNINGS GROWTH

By way of review we will comment briefly on the six causes of increases in earnings per share:

    I. Plow back of earnings.

        A major and regular cause of earnings increase.

   II. Sale of common stock above book value.

        A minor cause. The widespread fear that sale of stock will decrease earnings per share not necessarily justified.

  III. High price-earnings ratio company acquiring a low price-earnings ratio company in a stock swap.

        May have a major effect, but is strictly a one shot affair.

  IV. Increase in rate of return on common book value.

        A major cause, but there is a limit to which the return can be increased. To the extent that the new level of return continues to hold, with no change in percentage payout of dividends, there will be a permanently higher rate of growth in earnings per share from plow back.

   V.   Leverage.

        One way to increase the return on common book value and earnings per share with no change in return on long term capital. But debt can only be used up to a certain point, depending on the risk of the business, without adding unacceptable financial risk.

  VI. Retirement of Common Stock.

        A minor cause. This involves much more than the effect on the current earnings per share.

Finally, we have not answered the question but only raised it, whether increasing current earnings per share is a good management guide for making capital and financial decisions. We need a tool to answer that question adequately and that is what we will discuss in the next chapter.

TWO

HOW MANAGEMENT CAN MAKE

CORRECT CAPITAL DECISIONS

TO BENEFIT STOCKHOLDERS

WHICH STOCKHOLDERS MANAGEMENT
SHOULD AIM TO BENEFIT

In the introductory chapter we indicated that management may erroneously focus on trying to satisfy the short range whims of stockholders. Which stockholders should management concentrate on?

Individual stockholders have an ability that management does not have; they have fluidity of capital. If individual stockholders believe that earnings per share will turn down, they can sell their stock. Anyone who buys stock must have this possibility in mind.

Some stockholders may desire to be longer term investors than others. Some institutions in particular stress their desire to make long term investments almost to the point of giving the impression that they never have any intention of selling. They may indeed *wish* to be long term investors, but they would be doing a poor job if they did not watch for a possible down trend in earnings and sell before they believed it would occur.

A company, on the other hand, generally does not liquidate and return the capital to its stockholders; a company's stockholders never just evaporate.

Management must distinguish between the desires of any one stockholder or stockholder group at any one time and the desires of the whole body of stockholders over an extended period. Management represents all stockholders over the long run.

Therefore, there will be a continuous body of stockholders who must be satisfied during periods of both favorable and adverse earnings. This is the body of stockholders that management must have in mind in making decisions.

53

How can management benefit this body of stockholders when it makes capital and financial decisions? We suggest return on investment as the correct guide. To use it, we must know the minimum size that the return should be; the answer lies in the Cost-of-Capital. It is a complicated part of finance. The purpose and length of this book will not permit a complete discussion of Cost-of-Capital[1] but we will give enough information for an understanding of the subject and how it is applied. Before finishing the chapter we will show how the concept may be applied to acquisition pricing.

COST-OF-CAPITAL AND PROFIT GOALS

In order to lead up to our explanation of Cost-of-Capital let's see how our free enterprise profit economy works. To benefit consumers, competition should and does tend to drive prices down to the point where all costs are covered. Management should expand when there are prospects for a return greater than costs, and contract when costs are not covered. Costs should include a return sufficient to cover the Cost-of-Capital as measured in the competitive capital market, with due allowances for the risk of the investment.

We can start our explanation by referring to a simple balance sheet and a related income statement of a typical industrial company as shown in Table XIII. As a matter of fact, the figures shown in the table are an actual composite of all industrial companies in 1969. All figures are adjusted so that long term capital equals $100. There are many types of securities but the balance sheet is condensed to show the two basic types—debt and common equity. In Table XIII, long term capital consists of:

Debt	$ 23
Common equity	$ 77
Total	$100

[1] For a detailed discussion of Cost-of-Capital along with an explanation of how to calculate it, see *Profit Goals and Capital Management,* by John F. Childs, published by Prentice-Hall, Inc. 1968.

Cost of
Capital

Return on
Investment-
D.C.F.

Profit Goals

Earnings per Share

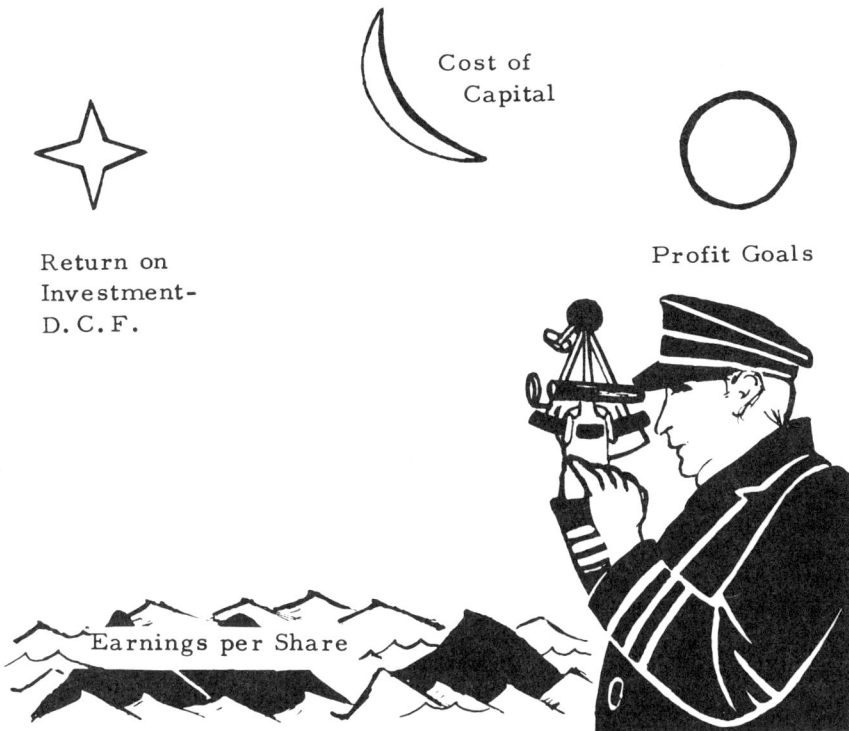

MANAGEMENT'S CAPITAL EXPENDITURE GUIDE.

The savings of our nation flow into corporations through long term capital—through the sale of debt, the sale of stock and from retained earnings. Retained earnings are a form of forced savings since the company decides not to pay out all the earnings in dividends.

The savers or investors want a return on both forms of long term capital. To put it another way, both forms of long term capital should be looked upon as having a cost from the company's point of view. Therefore, for Cost-of-Capital we need cost rates for each component in order to get an overall cost for long term capital.

COMMON COST

If we think of costs in terms of an income statement, as illustrated in Table XIII, it includes all costs, including the interest

Table XIII

FINANCIAL STATEMENTS FOR ALL INDUSTRIAL COMPANIES*
All figures adjusted on the basis of Long Term Capital equals 100

Part 1

BALANCE SHEET
December 31, 1969

Current Assets	$ 70	Current Liabilities		$ 35	THE SAVINGS OF
Plant, Net	56	Long Term Capital			OUR NATION FLOW
		Debt	$23		INTO CORPORATIONS
		Common Equity	77		THROUGH LONG TERM
		Total		100	CAPITAL—By the sale of
Other Items	14	Other Items		5	securities and from forced savings of retained earnings
Total	$140	Total		$140	

Part 2

INCOME STATEMENT
1969

Sales		$179	
Expenses			
Wages, Materials, etc.	$157		
Depreciation	6		
Interest†	1	- - - - - - - -	DEBT COST
Taxes	6		
Total expenses		170	ALL PROFIT—NO COST
Net Income for Common		$ 9	FOR COMMON CAPITAL??
Dividends		4	
Retained Earnings		$ 5	

$$\text{Return on Long Term Capital } after \text{ Taxes} = \frac{\$ 1 + \$ 9}{\$23 + \$77}$$

$$= 10\%$$

$$\text{Return on Common Book Value} = \frac{\$ 9}{\$77}$$

$$= 11.2\%$$

*For all manufacturing companies except newspapers, *Quarterly Financial Report for Manufacturing Corporations,* Federal Trade Commission—Securities and Exchange Commission. Figures for preferred stock are included with common equity, but the amount of preferred is relatively small.

†Estimated at 6%.

cost of debt capital, except for one cost—the cost of common equity capital. When we get to the bottom line, there is merely net income available for the common. No matter how little the income, it is shown as a profit. The common equity cost is the difficult part of Cost-of-Capital. One must understand that common equity does have a cost and how to measure it in order to understand the significance of return on capital figures.

There would be no question about all long term capital having a cost if a company's long term capital were all in the form of layers of senior and junior debt; the cost would be the interest rate. And the junior debt with no equity protection would have a very high interest cost. The mere fact that some long term capital is in the form of common equity does not mean that it does not have a cost.

Let's look at the cost of common equity from another angle. Suppose a company placed its pension plan with a financial institution and requested the institution to keep all of the funds invested in common stocks. Would not the company expect to receive a return from dividends and both realized and unrealized capital gains on the common stocks? If you asked a group of company officials this question, they would reply that they definitely expected a return and would probably give you an idea as to the rate. It might be from 10% to 15%. In turn, if the institution is going to generate a' return over the long run, *the companies represented by stocks in the portfolio must earn that return on their common equities.* For our entire economy, common stock investors can only receive what industry earns. Greater returns for a particular common stockholder can come only from picking the stocks of companies with better earnings or buying stocks which increase their price-earnings ratios. And any gain from a change in price-earnings ratio cannot be a continuous gain for all investors over an extended period.

The foregoing comments were intended to provide an appreciation that common equity does have an economic cost. Now we will define it.

> **Common equity cost is the relationship of the market price investors are willing to pay for a stock to the long range future benefits that they *expect* to receive.**

The future benefits come only from dividends and market appreciation, both of which come from earnings per share.

Calculating the common equity cost for a particular company is a difficult task because it involves an appraisal of the future benefits investors expect. However, for the purpose of this study we can use a relatively simple approach as follows: If our competitive economic system works well, as it appears to do, and, on the average, prices are driven down by competition to the point where all costs are just covered, then we can look to the broad average of what all industry earns on its common book value as a clue to common cost. For all industrial companies for the last ten years, the return on year end common book value is shown as 10.9%[2] or about 11% in Table XIV. We cannot use the figures of any individual company because it might be earning more or less than its common cost. And for the same reason, we cannot use the figures for any one industry.

The returns on book values for various companies at any one time tend to fit a bell shaped curve around this average of 11%. This can be seen in Table XV from the return on equity figures for the 500 largest companies reported in *Fortune* magazine. These figures show returns ranging from losses to over 20%. In 1969, the median return was 11.3%. The average of the medians for the last 10 years is 10.5%.

If, as stated above, our competitive economic system works well and on the average prices are driven down to the point where all costs are just covered, the average figure of about 11% may be a reasonable cost for common equity in the competitive capital market for a large conservatively capitalized company.

In our further discussion we will use this 11%[3] figure for that type of company. It is based on the last ten years when interest rates were at a relatively low level for most of the time compared with the rates in 1969. If interest rates persist near the 1969 levels it would be expected that investors would require a higher return on common.

The common cost may be approximately the same for large

---

[2]Average for ten years based on average of beginning and year end book value was 11.2%.

[3]In determining a complete Common Cost, an additional allowance should be made for the financing expenses connected with raising capital through the sale of stock.

Table XIV

RETURN ON YEAR END COMMON BOOK VALUE FOR INDUSTRIAL COMPANIES *

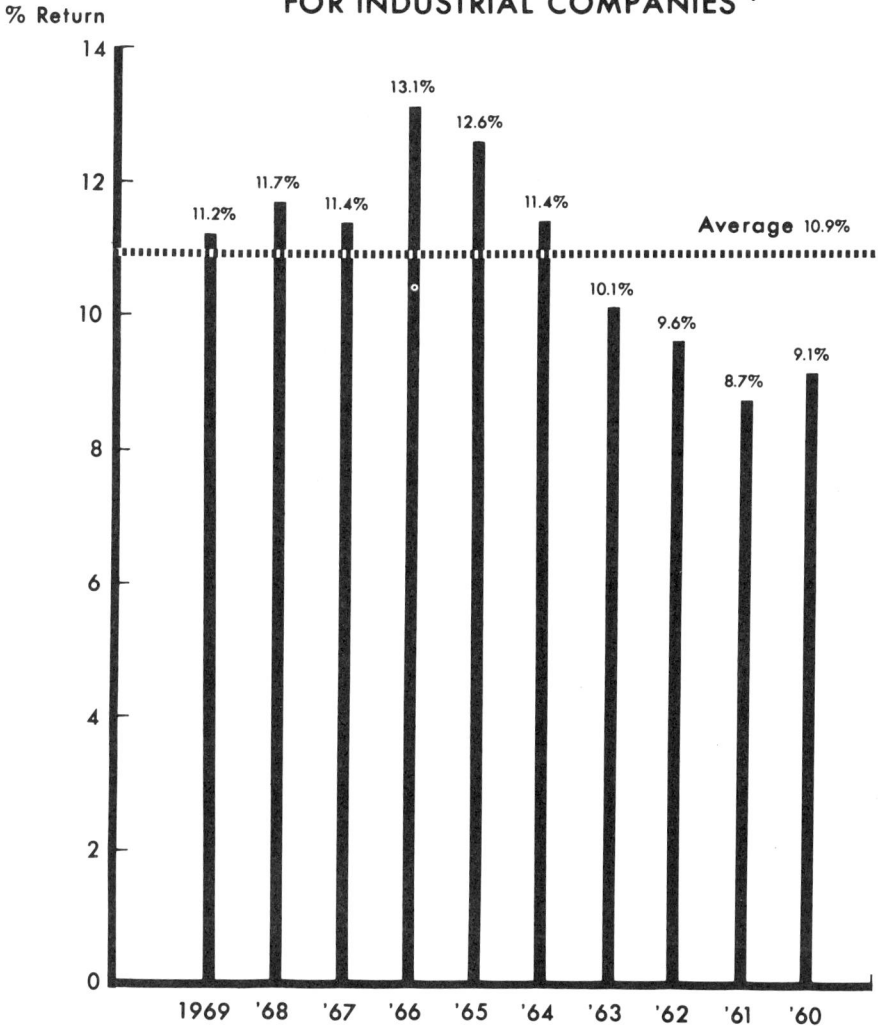

% Return

14 —

13.1%

12.6%

11.7%

11.2%   11.4%   11.4%   Average 10.9%
12 — ....

10.1%

10 —   9.6%   9.1%

8.7%

8 —

6 —

4 —

2 —

0 —

1969 '68 '67 '66 '65 '64 '63 '62 '61 '60

---

*For all manufacturing companies except newspapers, *Quarterly Financial Report for Manufacturing Corporations,* Federal Trade Commission–Securities and Exchange Commission. Figures for preferred stock are included with common equity, but the amount of preferred is relatively small.

Table XV

RETURN ON YEAR END EQUITY *
Number of 500 LARGEST COMPANIES IN FORTUNE SURVEY †
Companies

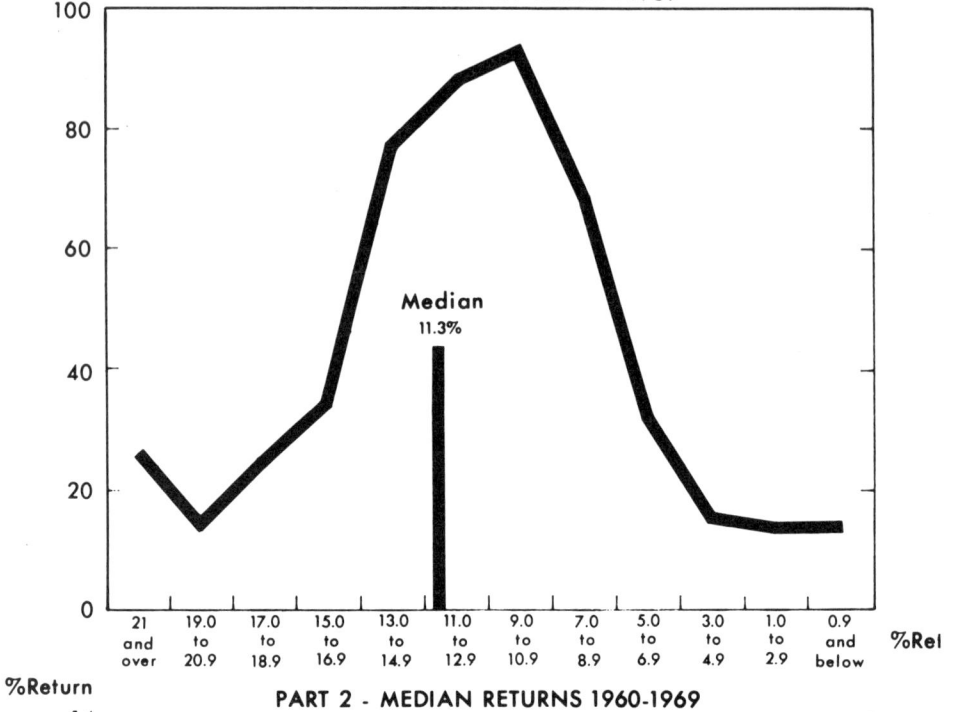

PART 1 - RANGE OF RETURN 1969

Median
11.3%

| 21 and over | 19.0 to 20.9 | 17.0 to 18.9 | 15.0 to 16.9 | 13.0 to 14.9 | 11.0 to 12.9 | 9.0 to 10.9 | 7.0 to 8.9 | 5.0 to 6.9 | 3.0 to 4.9 | 1.0 to 2.9 | 0.9 and below | %Rel |

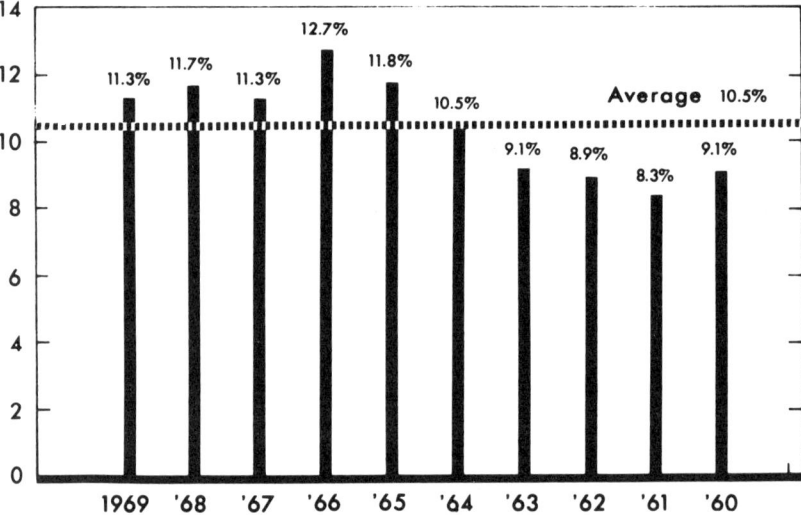

%Return
PART 2 - MEDIAN RETURNS 1960-1969

12.7%
11.3% 11.7% 11.3% 11.8%
10.5%   Average 10.5%
                        9.1% 8.9%   9.1%
                              8.3%

1969 '68 '67 '66 '65 '64 '63 '62 '61 '60

*Return on invested capital includes preferred stock, but preferred stock is relatively small, so that the figures are representative of the return on common equity.

†Reprinted from the Fortune Directory by permission; © 1969 Time, Inc.

companies which have different business risks because the debt levels can be varied so as to make the risk for the common comparable. The lower the business risk the greater amount of senior securities that can be used. This is illustrated in Table XVI for three types of business which have marked differences in risk. Industrial companies are more risky than electric utility companies and they are both more risky than finance companies. These rates are returns on capital. Returns on capital and Cost-of-Capital are not one and the same thing; however, they may coincide when broad averages are used.[4] Note that the returns on the common equities are relatively equal, but that the lower the risk the larger amount of senior securities that can be used and consequently the returns on long term capital tend to decrease.

It is, of course, possible for the risk of a business to be so great that even with no senior securities that the common cost would be higher than our 11% figure. This would apply particularly to smaller companies. Investors tend to regard companies with less than $100,000,000 in sales or assets as small companies, and consequently more risky investments. The size factor depends to some extent on the type of industry. The risk of the common equity and the rate required by investors also increase as a result of leverage; we discuss the question of leverage in Appendix C.

OVERALL COST-OF-CAPITAL

When we talk about the Cost-of-Capital for a particular capital investment, we are not referring to the cost of the security which may be used to finance that investment. That is an incremental cost approach which does not reflect the risk of the project as viewed by investors. For example, a plant may be financed with a bond issue; the cost rate for the bond is the interest rate. However, investors would not buy the bonds unless the company had some common

---

[4] As discussed in this chapter, the return on common equity for all industrial companies shown in Table XVI is sufficiently comprehensive to represent common cost. We do not suggest that this is true for the figures for the electric utility industry and finance companies. They represent single industries. Furthermore, the figures are for one year rather than an average over a period of years. The figures do, however, illustrate the point for which they are presented and they are used for that purpose only.

Table XVI

BUSINESSES WITH DIFFERENT RISKS.
RISKS FOR COMMON EQUITY APPROXIMATELY EQUATED THROUGH
VARIATIONS IN AMOUNT OF SENIOR SECURITIES

1969

Line Column	I	II	III	IV	V	VI	VII	VIII	IX
	Industrial Companies *			Electric Utility Industry†			Finance Companies‡		
Long Term Capital	Amount	Rate	Return	Amount	Rate	Return	Amount	Rate	Return
1 Senior Securities §	23%	6.0%	1.4%	64%	4.4%	2.8%	82%	6.0% ·	4.9%
2 Common Equity	77	11.2%	8.6	36	11.8%	4.2%	18	12.6	2.3
3 Total	100%		10.0%	100%		7.0%	100%		7.2%

Long Term Capital

| Senior Securities | Senior Securities | Senior Securities |
| Common 77% | Common 36% | Common 18% |

Return on Common Book Value

| 11.2% | 11.8% | 12.6% |

Return on Long Term Capital After Taxes

| 10.0% | 7.0% | 7.2% |

*For all manufacturing companies except newspapers, *Quarterly Financial Report for Manufacturing Corporations,* Federal Trade Commission—Securities and Exchange Commission. Figures for preferred stock are included with common equity but the amount of preferred is relatively small.

†Privately owned Electric Utilities—*Edison Electric Institute Statistical Book* 1969.

‡Four major finance companies as reported in Moody's Investors Service, Inc.

§Senior securities include long term debt and preferred stock for electric utility industry and finance companies. The rates on the senior securities are low because many of them were sold when interest rates were low.

equity to protect the bonds. A proper share of the company's common equity cost must be included in calculating the overall composite Cost-of-Capital.

Cost-of-capital is the composite weighted average cost of the various securities included in a company's capital structure measured over a period of time. It is representative of the risk of the business as viewed by investors.

In calculating Cost-of-Capital, average rates for the various securities over a period of five or ten years should be used. Because of the variability of the securities markets, spot or short range costs may not be typical of the costs a company and its competitors would experience under average representative market conditions.

Let's review the idea of Cost-of-Capital. Holders of senior securities have a rate of return they require to compensate them for the hire of their money and the risk they assume: the interest rate on debt and the dividend rate on preferred.[5] Similarly, common stockholders require a rate of return on their investment based on their appraisal of risk. If they do not get it they will sell their stock down to a price where the earnings represent the rate they require. For example, if stockholders require a 10% return and they believe the company only has prospects of earning $5 on $100 of common book value, stockholders will only pay $50. The $100 of investment is now worth only $50 in the market.

The overall Cost-of-Capital gives the company a standard of what it must earn on its capital as an absolute minimum to justify capital investments with risks equivalent to the overall risk of the company.

COST-OF-CAPITAL AND PROFIT GOAL
FOR LARGE INDUSTRIAL COMPANY

The Cost-of-Capital for a large conservatively capitalized industrial company is illustrated in Table XVII. The division between debt

---

[5] In the Introduction, it was indicated that the components to use in calculating the returns on capital for convertible debentures and convertible preferred are interest and dividends respectively. However, for Cost-of-Capital purposes, the common cost should be used for convertibles, otherwise there will not be sufficient earnings to cause conversion.

and common equity is about the same as that shown in Table XIII and XVI for all industrial companies. There is also included in Table XVII an allowance above Cost-of-Capital to arrive at a minimum Profit Goal. The relationship of Cost-of-Capital to a Profit Goal rate will be discussed later in this chapter. The rates shown in Column III are rates paid to investors and consequently are called To Investor Rates. They relate both the full interest rate paid to debt holders and the company's net income after taxes to long term capital. But the effect of interest on taxes reduces the rate the company must earn on its capital investments to satisfy these requirements. There are two other basic rates, the Pre-tax Rate and the After Tax Equivalent Rate, which are shown in Table XVII assuming a 50% tax rate.

Table XVII
COST-OF-CAPITAL AND MINIMUM PROFIT GOAL
FOR LARGE CONSERVATIVELY CAPITALIZED INDUSTRIAL
COMPANY

Column	I	II	III	IV	V
					50 % Tax Rate
Line			To Investor	Pre-Tax	After Tax
Long Term Capital Amount		Rate	Rate	Rate	Equivalent Rate
1 Debt	20%	6%*	1.20%	1.20%	0.60%
2 Common Equity	80	11	8.80	17.60	8.80
3 Total	100%		10.00%	18.80%	9.40%
4 Allowance Above Cost			2.00	4.00	2.00
5 Minimum Profit Goal			12.00%	22.80%	11.40%

*The average yield for Moody's Investors Service, Inc. A grade outstanding industrial bonds was 5.85% for the five years 1965-1969 and 5.15% for the ten years 1960-1969. When a company sells a new issue of bonds, the yield will have to be higher in order to induce the market to absorb the new issue. In addition, there will be financing costs which the company has to pay.

The Pre-tax Rate is as the name implies before taxes and all return for the long term capital.

The After Tax Equivalent Rate shows interest charges on a net basis after giving effect to the tax deductibility of interest. It is lower than the To Investor Rate to the extent of the tax savings.

The rate to use depends on the purpose for which it is intended:

To Investor Rate—This rate is used in determining whether the return which a company earns on long term capital, as calculated from figures in the income statement and balance sheet, is adequate to compensate all classes of security holders. It is comparable with return on long term capital *after* taxes as defined in Table I and shown in Table XIII.

Pre-tax Rate—A company may wish to use this rate as a measure of operating performance.

After Tax Equivalent Rate—This rate is used for comparison with the forecast profitability rate of a capital investment. In the analysis of a project, the income is generally calculated after taxes on a fully taxed basis, without any tax savings from interest. If the company has raised some of its capital in the form of debt, there will be some interest which will reduce the company's taxes. The investment should share in this tax saving. The after-tax equivalent rate reduces the goal rate to allow for this factor.

RISK EVALUATION

One of the major problems in establishing the proper Cost-of-Capital consists of evaluating the risk factor. The measurement of risk must come from the securities markets, because the market represents the views of investors who provide the capital. For many companies it is difficult and even impossible to obtain market evidence of Cost-of-Capital. This particularly applies to privately owned companies. Where evidence is not available, judgment—backed by a broad knowledge of Cost-of-Capital for various types of business—must be used. Not only may the overall rate vary from company to company, but a company should use different rates internally to allow for significant differences in risk for various divisions and capital expenditures.

Managements sometimes throw up their hands and say they cannot handle the risk factor. This is largely due to the fact that they do not understand the concept of Cost-of-Capital in the first place. A person knowledgeable in the field can generally come up with figures which are within the ball park for the desired purpose.

PROFIT GOAL ABOVE COST-OF-CAPITAL

A company should set its Profit Goal above its Cost-of-Capital; how much above has to be a matter of judgment. In Table XVII, we have allowed a minimum of 2%. Some industrial companies set their Profit Goals as high as 20% after taxes. Some of the factors to consider are as follows:

1. A company should try to achieve a return on long term capital above Cost-of-Capital in order to make a true economic profit.
2. Not all capital expenditures provide a return—parking lots and lunchrooms are examples.
3. Some companies may raise their Profit Goals to allow for errors in forecasting. As a practical matter, this may be a quick way to handle risk, but it may also lead to poor decisions. The risk of poor forecasting might better be handled by testing the key assumptions in the forecasts themselves.

How far a company's Profit Goal should be set above its Cost-of-Capital will have to be determined by management taking into account the above factors; no set rule can be formulated. No outside analyst is in a position to appraise the relevant internal factors. Too high a goal may price the company out of the market, or invite too much competition. Too low a goal will mean inadequate earnings.

APPLICATION OF PROFIT GOALS

In order to apply a Profit Goal in capital decision making, management must estimate the after tax rate of return on a capital investment over its life, with allowance for the time value of money. There are various "discounted cash flow" methods for calculating the return on investment for a project giving effect to the time value of money. One is known as Internal Rate of Return; another is Present Value. Articles and books[6] have covered the various methods.

This rate of return should then be compared with an After Tax

---

[6] See *Profit Goals and Capital Management* by John F. Childs, published by Prentice Hall Inc., 1968. Chapter XV, Profitability Rate written by Dr. Victor H. Brown, Partner, Touche, Ross, Bailey & Smart.

Equivalent Profit Goal in order to make a decision as to whether the project should be accepted.

The effect on earnings per share of the earnings flow from the investment should be calculated. This is required in order to determine the possible effect it might have on the market price of the stock. If a project is large in relation to the size of the company and has a long start up period, it might have a temporary adverse effect on earnings per share and market price. This should not be the basis for making a decision about the investment but if the company were in poor financial condition or the investment were a marginal one, it could carry some weight. In any case, management should be aware of the impact on earnings per share.

PROFIT GOALS RELATED TO ASSETS

Up until now we have talked only about the return related to long term capital. The investment base on which the return is calculated is important, because it affects the required rate. Management may prefer using some group of assets. Whatever base is used, the correct return should be related to it in order to provide an adequate return on long term capital. This can be illustrated with a simple balance sheet.

BALANCE SHEET

Current Assets	$100	Current Liabilities		$ 50
Plant, net	50	Long term Capital		
		Debt	$20	
		Common Equity	80	
		Total		$100
Total	$150	Total		$150

A return on long term capital of 10% after taxes is the same as a 10% return on working capital of $50 (current assets $100 less current liabilities $50) plus plant of $50 or a total of $100. Long term capital of $100 in this example supplies working capital and plant. However, if $50 of plant above is used as the base, the return would have to be 20% in order to provide 10% on long term capital. If the base is total assets of $150, then the return would only have to be 6 2/3% in order to be equivalent to 10% on long term capital. This switch from the right hand side of the balance sheet to the left is also critical in establishing divisional Profit Goals for a company.

There is nothing wrong with expressing Profit Goals based on other than long term capital so long as they are consistent. However, the place to start is with the return on long term capital. Any other criteria can be related to this basic goal.

RETURN ON SALES AS A GOAL

Some mangements pay close attention to return on sales. It is a useless goal, in itself, because the return on sales depends on capital turnover consistent with the nature of a business. The so-called DuPont formula[7] explains this point. The following illustration applies the DuPont formula to the composite figures for all industrial companies in 1969 as shown in Table XIII.

$$\frac{Sales}{Capital} \quad x \quad \frac{Return}{Sales} \quad = \quad \frac{Return}{Capital}$$

$$\frac{\$179}{\$100} \quad x \quad \frac{\$\ 10}{\$179} \quad = \quad \frac{\$\ 10}{\$100}$$

$$179\% \quad x \quad 5.6\% \quad = \quad 10\%$$

Thus an average industrial company in 1969 had $1.79 in sales per dollar of long term capital, it made 5.6% on sales, and had a 10% return on long term capital.

The amount of capital required per dollar of sales affects the percent that must be earned on sales in order to achieve a specific return on capital. It varies from industry to industry. For example, the cement industry requires a large amount of capital, and can only achieve about $1 of sales per $1 of capital. Therefore, to make a 10% return on capital would require a 10% return on sales. These figures are as follows:

$$\frac{Sales}{Capital} \quad x \quad \frac{Return}{Sales} \quad = \quad \frac{Return}{Capital}$$

$$\frac{\$100}{\$100} \quad x \quad \frac{\$\ 10}{\$100} \quad = \quad \frac{\$\ 10}{\$100}$$

$$100\% \quad x \quad 10\% \quad = \quad 10\%$$

[7] Reprinted by permission of E. I. DuPont de Nemours & Co., Wilmington, Delaware 19898 from its publication, Executive Committee Control Charts.

The important point is to establish a return on sales goal which is consistent with both the sales-to-capital relationship and the return-on-capital goal.

CONFLICTING GOALS

Some companies set corporate goals which conflict. For example, here is a set of goals for capital investment and acquisitions set by one company which has a dividend payout policy of 50%.

> **Earn 10% on sales after taxes**
> **Earn 15% on common equity**
> **Have a growth rate in earnings per share of 15% per year**

We have already explained why percent on sales is meaningless unless the capital intensity of the business is also defined. The 15% return on common book value and a 15% growth rate in earnings per share with a 50% payout in dividends is inconsistent. With a 15% return on common book value as well as a fixed dividend payout, the growth rate in earnings per share would be 7 1/2% (15% earned on common book value multipled by 50% of earnings retained). If the management expected to achieve a permanent 15% growth in earnings per share with a 50% payout, the return on common equity goal would have to be 30%.

As far as the return on common book value is concerned, the leverage or proportion of debt in the capital structure makes a major difference, and the amount of debt depends on the risk of the business. A return on common book value of 15% for a highly leveraged company is nothing to brag about. Thus, in establishing a return on common, it is also necessary to define the percentage of senior securities in long term capital; it may be preferable to use a return on long term capital.

ACQUISTION PRICING RELATED TO PROFIT GOALS

An acquisition is one form of capital investment; it is an indirect investment in the assets of a going concern. And yet managements tend to use entirely different rules in appraising an acquisition than they do in appraising a capital investment in assets.

As a matter of fact, the acquisition craze has brought to the surface some of the worst in American management. Basically, there are four groups who are acquisition minded:

1. The financial manipulators
2. The sheep
3. The scared ones
4. The doers

The financial manipulators are the ones who play the game of increasing current earnings per share. They boost their price-earnings ratio by every means possible in order to buy lower price-earnings ratio companies and further extend their false high price-earnings ratio. They may use all kinds of complicated securities with excessive leverage. The only ones who benefit in this game in the long run are the management promoters. Our economy is not benefited in any way and the poor investors ultimately pay the price.

The sheep are the poor innocents who are in the game because it is the thing to do. They fear that they will be looked down on if they are not in the action.

The scared ones are those unfortunates who are vulnerable to being taken over—perhaps through their own fault. Perhaps not. They get almost panicky to grab someone else in order to add glamour to their company and get up their price-earnings ratio in order to stave off a tender offer.

The doers are the only ones who are being constructive. Their approach is to improve the companies they take over in order to provide better products and thus earn more money. This helps our economy and everyone concerned, provided the anti-trust laws are not violated and the acquisitions make sense from a long range managerial point of view.

It is amusing to note the criteria that some acquisition minded companies establish, such as: growth in sales 10%, return on common 15%, and excellent management. If a company is that good, it probably should be doing the acquiring rather than be acquired. These might be satisfactory goals for an acquiring company to have in mind as to what it should do with the acquired company in the future. However, anyone would have to be daydreaming to believe that many such currently successful companies were readily available for purchase at a reasonable price.

There are two prices in any acquisition: What has to be paid and what the acquisition is worth. Generally, only the first is considered even by the acquiring company. What has to be paid for an acquisition depends on the demand and supply for the type of company being acquired. If there is a seller's market, the price that has to be paid may well be out of line. The price will probably be stated in terms of a price-earnings ratio for the common as compared to price-earnings ratios of similar stocks, with allowances for differences in the companies being compared.

There has been much controversy over the way an acquisition is accounted for–pooling or purchase. The method of accounting does not determine the price to be paid. It will affect the timing of the bookkeeping earnings per share, but not the true return on invested capital. In fact, if an acquisition makes sense from the point of view of return on investment, it may be even better with purchase accounting than with pooling treatment, because purchase accounting may provide an added tax benefit from the write up and subsequent redepreciation of some of the assets. However, because some managements erroneously use earnings per share as a guide for decision making, pooling may appear indispensable in acquisition decision making.

Generally, the same principle should be used to appraise an acquisition as to appraise investment in assets, although the calculations may be more complicated. Acquisition appraisal involves making an estimate of the amount that can be paid and still produce a satisfactory Profit Goal over an extended period.

If a company is going to acquire the common stock of another company, it should proceed as follows:

1. Identify assets that can be liquidated which are not needed to carry on operations and determine their present after tax value.
2. Make an estimate of cash flow before taxes and interest, based on all considerations as to what the company would like after it was acquired.
3. Deduct taxes from the forecast pre-tax income at the full tax rate.
4. Add new capital expenditures for plant and working capital which will be required in order to generate the forecast sales and earnings.
5. Carry the forecast out for a sufficiently long period of time and

place a terminal value on the company at the end of the period. The length of period may be 5, 10, 15 years or longer, depending on the circumstances.

6. Consider the effect of the acquired company's operations on the operations of the acquiring company. This may have to be included in the forecast.

7. Calculate the present worth of the stream of after tax cash flows, capital expenditures and terminal value, discounted at the after-tax equivalent Profit Goal rate which justifies the investment.

8. The result will be the maximum amount of long term capital which can be invested to make the acquisition.

9. Subtract the existing long term debt from the total present value to obtain the value of the common stock which is being purchased. This approach avoids the danger of being deceived by high earnings on common stock of a company where the capital structure is highly leveraged. This, plus the after tax value of excess assets as determined in step one, is the amount that can be paid for the acquisition.

These calculations are not simple. Tax questions may be knotty and various special factors may arise. It may be advisable to make two or three forecasts with different assumptions.

The effect of changes in critical expense items, critical capital expenditures and terminal values must be tested. Terminal values, based on asset value, going concern value and liquidating value, may be tested. If such a study is made and carefully examined, it should be possible to come up with a figure as to the approximate worth of the acquisition.

Because such forecasts may have to be for a number of years ahead, it may appear that the forecasts are of little value. Furthermore, any terminal value placed on the acquired company a number of years hence may be only a best guess. Fortunately, as far as a terminal value is concerned there is a partial saving grace: discounting makes values further out have less effect on the overall return.

Before you throw up your hands in disbelief at the value of such forecasts, you should consider their purpose. Their primary purpose is to provide a picture of figures that might unfold so that the management can ask themselves whether the figures are within the realm of possibility in view of such factors as: the premium over sound asset value which has to be paid, the new capital which has to be added, the sales which have to be generated, the major expense items, the profit margin on sales, and the possible value of the investment at some future time. Such a study will indicate some of the risks that will have to be taken and what might happen if the acquisition turns sour and becomes a millstone around the acquirer's neck. Also, it might help the company think through the question of whether the acquiring company could better enter the field by starting up such a business on its own.

This completes our discussion of the guide for management decision making which we suggest instead of current earnings per share. Return on investment and Profit Goals are no simple subjects. No matter what purpose they are used for, they must be thoroughly understood in order to avoid unsound judgments. But properly applied they are the correct approach for capital decision making. In the next chapter we will see why this is so.

THREE

WHY CURRENT EARNINGS PER SHARE

ARE A POOR MANAGEMENT GUIDE

After discussing each cause of increase in current earnings per share in Chapter One, we questioned whether an increase could be used as a guide for capital investments. For example:

What about an increase in current earnings per share from the more profitable use of assets?

What about an increase in current earnings per share due to external growth from a high price-earnings ratio company buying a low price-earnings ratio company in a stock swap?

In the last chapter, we suggested that Cost-of-Capital is the proper guide. We will now apply this tool in two examples which show how increasing current earnings per share is a poor guide for management decision making.

Example #1

A company has 1,000,000 common shares outstanding with net income of $4,000,000. Earnings per share are $4.00. Part of its assets consist of $10,000,000 invested in short term investments providing a pre-tax return of 5% and an after-tax return (assuming a 50% tax rate) of 2 1/2% or $250,000. This accounts for 25¢ of the $4.00 earnings per share.

	Total	Per Share
Shares outstanding	1,000,000	
Net income	$ 4,000,000	$4.00
Temporary investment	$10,000,000	
Income from temporary investment after taxes (2 1/2%)	$ 250,000	-0.25
New capital investment	$10,000,000	
Income from new capital investment	$ 800,000	+0.80
Resulting earnings per share		$4.55

The company decides to sell the short term investments and spend the proceeds on a capital investment which will produce an 8% annual return after all expenses, including depreciation and taxes, for the life of the investment. To make the calculations simple, we will assume that the depreciation is reinvested at the same rate for the life of the project. This project will produce $800,000 of earnings after taxes. This will represent 80¢ per share of common stock as compared with the 25¢ per share obtained on the short term investments. The total earnings per share will increase from $4.00 to $4.55.

On the surface this looks good. However, if the risk in the project required a 10% return, based on Cost-of-Capital, rather than 8%, the $10,000,000 investment in the project would only be worth $8,000,000. Only at the $8,000,000 figure could investors obtain a 10% return to compensate them for the risk since the project will earn only $800,000. Furthermore, if the company decided to sell the project, a knowledgeable buyer would only pay $8,000,000 because if he paid more he would receive less than a 10% return. Thus, while current earnings per share increased, the company actually lost $2,000,000 of capital by making the investment. Ultimately, this bad investment, with a return below the return required to cover all costs in view of the risk involved, will have to be reflected in the market price of the stock. This is true in spite of the fact that the market price of the stock undoubtedly would be favorably affected in the short run, since current earnings per share increase.

The company should have left the money invested in the temporary investment until it found a project which would produce more than the Cost-of-Capital. While the return on the temporary investment is lower, the return is commensurate with the risk. An investment of $10,000,000 in short term U. S. Treasury securities is *worth* $10,000,000. Because of lack of investor understanding, the company's market price may suffer *temporarily* because a substantial portion of its capital is earning at a low rate in money market investments. However, cash can always be pulled out of short term riskless investments if a good expenditure proposal comes along. The company's stock will suffer *permanently* if it invests in a capital project below Cost-of-Capital. If the company does not want to reserve the money until a worthwhile project comes along, it should pay it out to its stockholders. Certainly, it should not make an investment on which it would realize a capital loss even though current earnings per share increased.

Perhaps the following analogy might be helpful. Suppose an investor wanted to invest $10,000,000 in bonds rated BBB quality by the bond rating agencies. Assume that this investor was like some executives who make capital investments and did not understand the return he should get in view of the risk involved. In 1969, a BBB bond should provide a return of about 10% to an investor. However, follow our assumption: The investor did not appraise the risk properly and as a result invested the $10,000,000 with only an 8% interest. He in fact only got bonds worth about $8,000,000, because that is all any investor who understood risk and rate would be willing to pay for the bonds. At $8,000,000 with an annual interest of $800,000, the return would be approximately 10%. The same thing happens when a company makes a capital investment below the Cost-of-Capital even though current earnings per share increase.

The conclusion with regard to our capital investment example above would not have been different if funds were obtained from any other source than short term investments–cash, sale of senior securities, financed with a lease, or sale of common stock. The capital investment must produce earnings to cover more than its risk. The method of financing is one question and the return required on the capital investment is another separate question.

Example #2

Now let's look at an acquisition which will increase current earnings per share. Company A's stock is selling for 20 times earnings. It wishes to acquire the common stock of Company B for $30,000,000 which is 15 times company B's earnings of $2,000,000. Company B does not care how it gets paid.

Therefore, Company A has the following possible methods to use to acquire it.

1. With $30,000,000 market value of its own stock.
2. With the proceeds from the sale of $30,000,000 of 8% bonds with a net interest cost of 4% after allowing for a 50% tax rate.

3. With the proceeds from the sale of $30,000,000 of temporary investments which earn 5% interest and provide a 2½% return after taxes (assuming a 50% tax rate).

No matter what method is used current earnings per share will be increased. Company A has a higher price-earnings ratio than Company B, and the earnings-purchase price percentage of Company B is 6 2/3% which is more than the 4% net interest cost of the bond issue and more than the 2½% net interest received on the temporary investment. Also no matter what method is used, Company A is paying $30,000,000 for Company B.[1]

Company B's long term capital consists of 100% common equity with a common book value of $10,000,000 after the balance sheet has been adjusted to represent current values for the various items. This should always be done so that the buying company knows what it is getting in terms of real assets. To reiterate, net income after taxes amounted to $2,000,000 and the purchase price is $30,000,000, which is 15 times earnings. Thus Company A would be paying a premium over real asset value of $20,000,000, which is termed goodwill. We will assume that the minimum Profit Goal on this capital investment is 12% so that earnings on the $30,000,000 would have to be $3,600,000. This is quite an increase over the $2,000,000 which Company B is earning currently. Furthermore, earnings after taxes of $3,600,000 would represent a 36% return on the real asset value of $10,000,000. Who can make that in our

Company B

Long Term Capital Common book value	$10,000,000
Net income for common after taxes	$ 2,000,000
Return on common book value	20%
Purchase price for all common	$30,000,000
Price earnings ratio	15
Premium over sound common book value—goodwill	$20,000,000
Minimum return required on purchase price	12%
Minimum earnings required	$ 3,600,000
Required earnings as a percent of sound book value	36%

---

[1] This assumes that if Company A used its own stock, it would have the alternative of selling that amount of stock in the market for approximately $30,000,000.

competitive economy? Competitors would be setting prices to cover expenses and a return on their actual assets invested; consequently, they would be willing to accept a much lower profit than the buyer of Company B would need. Company A should consider whether it could go into the business on its own. It would be just as well off to spend $10,000,000 to duplicate the assets and $20,000,000 on start up costs, etc., to produce the results it would have gotten from acquiring Company B.

Now, however, let's change the picture. Suppose that this original investment made it possible for Company A to get into a business in which it could put a large additional investment of $100,000,000. Then the earnings requirement based on the same tests would be as follows:

	With Premium	Without Premium
Common stock book value with assets stated at current value	$ 10,000,000	$ 10,000,000
Premium paid–goodwill	20,000,000	
New investment to be added	100,000,000	100,000,000
Total	$130,000,000	$110,000,000
Earnings goal for success–12%	$15,600,000	$15,600,000
Required return on capital less premium		14%

The 14% return on capital less premium might be hard to achieve in our competitive economy, but it may, at least, be within the realm of possibility. It is quite different from the 36% which would have to be earned on the actual assets if the acquisition did not represent an opportunity to make an additional investment. And yet using increasing current earnings per share as a guide would have suggested that the acquisition was justified even without the possibility of making an additional investment. Therefore, we have to fall back on our guide of a Profit Goal in order to make a correct decision.

A company which is in a good position to raise common equity capital by selling stock near its market price makes a serious mistake in acquiring another company for stock if the acquisition offers a projected return on the *market value of the shares issued* below a fair Profit Goal. The acquirer has the option of foregoing the acquisition, selling shares for cash instead, and investing this cash to earn an adequate return on the market value of the shares sold.

COMPANIES WITH "CHINESE MONEY" STOCK

However, companies with overvalued, "Chinese money" stock may not be able to offer stock for cash in the market in quantity, perhaps not even at all, without severely depressing the price. The stock may be largely in weak hands, and any temporary dilution in earnings per share from a proposed offering may prompt the holders to dump it. Under these circumstances, a company might be better off overpaying—in "Chinese money"—for an acquisition than not making it at all.

Suppose Company X's stock has a market price of $100. Further suppose that it would have a market price of $40, its "real" value, if investors understood its prospects and its risks thoroughly. It is considering acquiring Company Y, which has a "real" value of $30 and a market price of $30. Company Y could be bought for $40 in market price of Company X's stock. The price-earnings ratio of Company X is higher than the purchase price-earnings ratio of Company Y so that with a pooling of interests, current earnings per share will increase as a result of the acquisition to $5.00.

Company X	-	Market price	$100
		"Real " value	$ 40
		Earnings per share	$ 4
		Price-earnings ratio	25
Company Y	-	Market price	$ 30
		Purchase price	$ 40
		"Real" value	$ 30
		Earnings per share	$ 3
		Purchase price-earnings ratio	13 1/3

If X does not buy Y, X's stock may collapse to its "real" value of $40. If X does buy Y the following might happen on a per share basis, assuming each company has an equal number of shares outstanding before the acquisition.

1. Company X issues 0.4 shares with a market value of $40 to acquire each share of Company Y.
2. After the acquisition, the market collapses to the "real" values—Company X "real" value $40 plus Company Y "real" value $30 for a total "real" value $70.
3. Company X has outstanding 1.4 shares for every $70 of "real" value. This is equivalent to a "real" value of $50.00 per share ($70 ÷ 1.4 = $50.00).

When the market recognizes "real" values, the stock of Company X falls from $100 to $50.00 rather than $40.

Of course, the stockholders of Company Y suffer as a result of this transaction—the gain by Company X's stockholders has come at the expense of Company Y's. The stock exchanged for Company Y would be worth only $20.00 per share ($50.00 "real" value of new shares x 0.4 shares) rather than its former "real" value of $30. A rather sad situation for our economy as a whole. A company should be run more constructively and find a better alternative than to have to resort to this type of operation. But some companies have followed this policy when they found suckers such as Company Y.

INCREASING EXISTING RETURN ON CAPITAL ALSO A POOR GUIDE

We have concentrated our discussion on increasing current earnings per share as a guide. Sometimes, management uses an increase of the existing return on capital as a guide. It is also an unreliable guide. Look at the simple example shown in Table XVIII, Part 1. In this case, the project would increase the return on long term capital, but since the return on the new capital of 9% is below the Profit Goal it should be rejected. And since it is below the Cost-of-Capital, there would actually be a loss of capital if it were accepted. This would be reflected in adverse market performance for the stock in the long run.

Table XVIII

RELATIONSHIP OF RETURN ON NEW CAPITAL TO RETURN ON OLD CAPITAL—NO GUIDE FOR CAPITAL DECISION MAKING

Part 1

HIGHER RETURN ON NEW CAPITAL BUT BELOW COST-OF-CAPITAL

Return on existing Long Term Capital	8%
Expected return on new project	9%
Cost-of-Capital—common cost	10%
Profit Goal for new project	12%

Column	I Shares	II Total	III Per Share	IV Return	V Total	VI Per Share	VII Ratio	VIII of Common
Line		Long Term Capital—All Common			Earnings		P/E	Market Price
1	10	$1,000	$100	8.0%	$80.00	$8.000	10	$80.00
2 New	1	80	80	9.0	7.20			
3	11	$1,080		8.1%	$87.20	$7.927	10	$79.27

Part 2

LOWER RETURN ON NEW CAPITAL BUT ABOVE COST-OF-CAPITAL

Return on existing Long Term Capital	20%
Expected return on new project	15%
Cost-of-Capital—common cost	10%
Profit Goal for new project	12%

Column	I Shares	II Total	III Per Share	IV Return	V Total	VI Per Share	VII Ratio	VIII of Common
Line		Long Term Capital—All Common			Earnings		P/E	Market Price
1	10	$1,000	$100	20.0%	$200	$20.00	10	$200.00
2 New	1	200	200	15.0	30			
3	11	$1,200		19.2%	$230	$20.91	10	$209.10

On the other hand, a company can take on projects with a lower return than the company's existing return and still benefit its stockholders, provided the return is above the Cost-of-Capital. A simple example shown in Table XVIII, Part 2 will explain. If the company accepts the project and it materializes as anticipated, the return on the long term capital for the company will decrease. However, provided the return on the old investment does not change, the stockholders will benefit, because there will be an additional profit on the new investment above all costs including the Cost-of-Capital. This gain will be reflected favorably in the market price of the common stock in the long run.

The end result of this table is due to two separate things: One, new capital is invested at a rate different from Cost-of-Capital and two, capital is raised at a price other than book value.

Another example, based on reinvestment of retained earnings, is shown below with the same assumptions used in Table XVIII, where the Cost-of-Capital is 10%.

Part I

Year	Shares	Common Book Value		Return	Earnings	Price-Earnings Ratio	Market Price
1	1	$100		8%	$ 8.00	10	$ 80.00
2	Reinvestment of retained earnings	8 Below C-O-C		9%	0.72	10	7.20
3		$108		8.1%	$ 8.72	10	87.20

Part 2

Year	Shares	Common Book Value		Return	Earnings	Price-Earnings Ratio	Market Price
1	1	$100		20%	$20.00	10	$200.00
2	Reinvestment of retained earnings	20 Above C-O-C		15%	3.00	10	30.00
3		$120		19.2%	$23.00	10	$230.00

In both parts, earnings per share increased due to plow back. However, the new investment of $8 in Part 1 is only worth $7.20 in the market, invested above the rate on the old investment but below Cost-of-Capital. In Part 2, the new investment of $20 is worth $30 in the market, invested below the rate on the old investment but above Cost-of-Capital. Thus, in one case investors suffer a loss of the new capital, while in the other they gain.

EFFECT OF FAILURE TO COVER COST-OF-CAPITAL

What are the broader implications if a company expands and does not cover all costs, including the Cost-of-Capital, because it prefers to base expansion policies on some other criterion such as increasing current earnings per share, or increasing return on existing investment. There are three adverse results:

1. Its stockholders are hurt because they are not rewarded fairly.
2. Other companies in the industry suffer because excess capacity drives prices down and hurts their return on capital. This is not to suggest that knowledgeable competition should be stifled or feared but competition among companies which do not know their costs is destructive. Knowledge about capital costs is one of the weakest areas of management.
3. Our standard of living is adversely affected. If capital is put into production where there is already an adequate supply of goods, some of the capital of our country, which should be used to produce other needed goods, is misdirected and wasted.

In the next chapter we will give an example in another area of capital investment in which earnings per share can be a misleading guide.

FOUR

FROM NOTHING TO MILLIONS-

VENTURE CAPITAL COMPANIES

The venture capital field is wide open for the earnings per share game. New companies are started with relatively little capital in hopes that they will become another IBM and make millions. How these small firms grow will be the topic of this chapter. We will utilize the measures of earnings per share, price-earnings ratios and return on investment to illuminate the subject.

A typical venture is the new high technology firm which often has its origin in the mind of a scientist or engineer from a major firm who wants to develop his brain child and reap the rewards. Other, more pedestrian ventures which have gained recent popularity are food franchise operations and nursing homes. Those with acceptable credentials in a fashionable field apparently find little trouble raising money from wealthy individuals, speculative mutual funds, investment bankers and recently from such traditionally staid groups as banks and large corporations. Because brilliant scientists can be less than brilliant out of the laboratory, these firms may need considerable hand holding as well as considerable business advice during their early years. This is often supplied in part by those who provide the original capital.

Briefly, what happens may be like this. A new company is started with private investors putting up the seed money. The company finally gets off the ground and shows some prospects but needs more money. It is in a glamourous business and, while it may show little in the way of earnings per share, the public is nevertheless willing to pay a fantastic price for the stock. If the insiders want to get some of their money back, they have it made—they have a willing public on which to unload. A successful business, starting from such a small base may produce a very fast growth rate in earnings per share and consequently a stock with a high price-earnings ratio. However, in time, competition prevents the company from showing a high return on capital and finally, its growth is largely dependent on plow back of earnings. Growth in earnings slows down and the stock falls off in price. The company becomes just another small company selling at a low multiple of earnings, causing those who got in at high prices to lose their shirts. While exceptions prove to be great success stories, this is a tough game where amateurs get burned and the pros don't find it easy.

Pot of Gold

OR

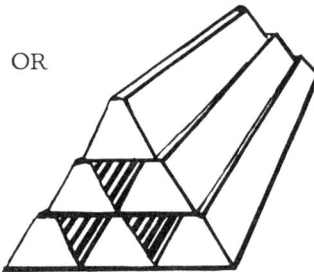

Gold Bricks

NEW VENTURES.

The *Institutional Investor* in an article "Venture Capital: The Biggest Mousetrap of the 1970's?"[1] summed up the results of venture capital with the following story about American Research and Development Corporation.

> Most venture capitalists keep their investment records quite confidential (though they do like to brag about winners), but one company whose achievements are known is the publicly-owned

---

[1] By Chris Welles, January, 1970.

American Research & Development Corp., which professes to maintain a close involvement with its investments and whose success has been widely acclaimed. AR&D has been called everything from "the most successful venture capital firm on record" (Forbes) to "the most preeminent venture capital company of modern times" which "has demonstrated the most golden touch in industry" (Dun's Review). However, in a September-October 1968 article in the *Financial Analysts Journal,* William Rotch, professor of business administration at the University of Virginia's Graduate School of Business Administration, concluded that during the first 20 years of AR&D's operation through the beginning of 1967 "recognizing income and capital gains dividends when declared and assuming all unrealized gains were realized and distributed on December 31, 1966, the stockholder's investment would have resulted in approximately a 14 percent compounded annual return." Without Digital Equipment, by far the most successful of all of the 100 companies in which AR&D has invested, the return fell to only 8 percent. By contrast, the Dow Jones Industrial Average over the same period, assuming a 4½ percent dividend yield, showed a compounded annual return of about 11½ percent.

In order to show how this game works in terms of earnings per share, price-earnings ratio and return on capital, we will outline some figures for a hypothetical company we will call Nothing Ventured Nothing Gained Company, or NVNG Co. New ventures may involve complicated capital structures with warrants, stock options and high leverage. When the companies go public, they may be doomed to failure not only because of financing methods, but also because of the excessive share which the promoters allocate to themselves. The financing for NVNG Co. will be kept relatively simple so as not to over-complicate the picture.

HOW A NEW COMPANY STARTS

Table XIX, shows how NVNG Co. starts out with $2,000,000 of common equity provided by private investors. The return on common book value goes from 1% to 8% in four years. While 8% is a low return, the increase in return on common book value, combined with the added growth from plow back, produces a very high growth rate in earnings per share. The company now needs more money.

Table XIX

NOTHING VENTURED NOTHING GAINED COMPANY

THE START

All Funds Generated in One Year Are Reinvested at the Beginning of the Next Year

Line		Year 1	Year 2	Year 3	Year 4	Year 5	Year 6
	Common Equity						
	No. of Shares						
1	Old	200,000	200,000	200,000	200,000	200,000	200,000
2	New					100,000	
3	Total					300,000	300,000
	Book Value						
4	Old	$2,000,000	$2,020,000	$2,060,400	$2,142,816	$2,314,241	$2,545,665
5	New					2,700,000*	2,700,000
6	Total					$5,014,241	$5,245,665
7	Per share	$10.00	$10.10	$10.30	$10.71	$16.71*	$17.49
	% Return on Common Book						
8	Value	1%	2%	4%	8%	10%	10%
	Earnings for Common Equity						
9	Total	$ 20,000	$ 40,400	$ 82,416	$ 171,425	$ 231,424	$ 524,567
10	Per Share	$0.10	$0.20	$0.41	$0.86	$0.77	$1.75

Line		Year 1	Year 2	Year 3	Year 4	Year 5	Year 6
11	Growth Rate in earnings per share		100%	105%	110%	-10%	127%
12	Price-Earnings Ratio						40
13	Market Price						$70
14	Market Price as % of Book Value						400%
	Common Stock Financing						
15	Secondary					100,000	
16	Primary					100,000	
	Original Owners Investment						
17	Original Investment	$2,000,000					
18	Sale of Stock					$2,700,000	
19	Market Value of Remaining Shares					$2,700,000	$7,000,000
20	Total					$5,400,000	$7,000,000

*Common sold in 5th year, but no return on this new capital until the 6th year.

93

With its great growth in earnings per share and its glamourous name, it is able to offer stock publicly in the fifth year at $27, which is 32 times the previous year's earnings of $0.86. The offering consists of two parts: 100,000 shares belonging to the original investors and 100,000 shares to provide new capital. The original owners thus get $2,700,000—which is more than they put in originally—and they still have 100,000 shares worth $2,700,000 at a price of $27. The 100,000 shares sold publicly provides the company with $2,700,000 of new capital for expansion.

The company earns 10% on its original investment in the fifth year and 10% on the total investment, including the new money in the sixth year. Earnings per share get a real boost in the sixth year due to the sale of stock above book value as well as plow back.

Thus in the sixth year the company has given the impression of being a world beater with earnings per share growth of over 100% per year except in the year of the common offering. As a consequence, investors are inspired, the price-earnings ratio is high and the stock sells for 400% of common book value.

Actually, however, the company is not yet earning the Cost-of-Capital on its common equity. The risk is such in this type of venture, that the common cost is probably well above 10%—furthermore, the common in all likelihood is highly leveraged with debt, adding to its risk. The debt part of the capital is not shown in the table. Thus the test of the company's ability is yet to come.

Looking at the future from a broad point of view, three things can happen: The company can be a failure, it can achieve mediocrity or it can be a success. In the next three tables, we show these possibilities in condensed form. Only three years are shown to make it simple. In all probability the story would not be told in so brief a time.

FAILURE

In Table XX, we show failure. The return on common has fallen off to 8% in year 9. Investors have lost interest and the stock is a dog at 8 times earnings. The public who came into the market at $27 would now have stock only worth $15. The promoters would still have 100,000 shares with a market value

Table XX

NOTHING VENTURED NOTHING GAINED COMPANY
FAILURE

All Funds Generated in One Year Are Reinvested at the Beginning of the Next Year

Line		Year 7	Year 8	Year 9
1	Common Equity			
	Number of Shares	300,000	300,000	300,000
2	Book value Per Share	$ 19.23	$ 21.16	$ 22.85
	Total	$5,770,232	$6,347,255	$6,855,035
3	% Return on common			
	book value	10%	8%	8%
4	Earnings for Common equity—			
5	Total	$ 577,023	$ 507,780	$ 548,403
6	Per Share	$ 1.92	$ 1.69	$ 1.83
7	Growth rate in earnings			
	per share	10%	-12%	8%
8	Price-earnings ratio	25	15	8
9	Market Price	$ 48	$ 25	$ 15
10	Market price as % of			
	book value	250%	118%	66%

of $1,500,000, but since they only put in $2,000,000 and already took out $2,700,000 they are not hurting.

MEDIOCRITY

In Table XXI, we show what would happen if NVNG Co. achieved mediocrity. The return on common equity has gone to 11%. The growth rate in earnings per share is now dependent entirely on plow back and with no dividend payments the growth rate is 11%. If as the company matures it pays out 50% of its earnings in dividends, the growth rate in earnings per share would only be 5½%. The stock sells for 11 times earnings and a little above book value.

A return of 11% on common book value is representative of the average return for large well established companies able to keep their heads above water in our highly competitive economy. This does not mean that all new ventures have a good chance of even landing up here. And this is not much solace to the public which bought the stock at a speculative price of $27 per share four years ago, received no dividends, and now finds the stock worth only $29. That is an annual return of less than 2% in four years.

Table XXI

NOTHING VENTURED NOTHING GAINED COMPANY

MEDIOCRITY

All Funds Generated in One Year Are Reinvested at the Beginning of the Next Year

Line		Year 7	Year 8	Year 9
1	Common equity			
	Number of shares	300,000	300,000	300,000
2	Book value Per Share	$ 19.23	$ 21.35	$ 23.70
3	Total	$5,770,232	$6,404,958	$7,109,503
4	% Return on common			
	book value	11%	11%	11%
	Earnings for common equity			
5	Total	$ 634,726	$ 704,545	$ 782,045
6	Per Share	$ 2.12	$ 2.35	$ 2.61
7	Growth rate in earnings			
	per share	21%	11%	11%
8	Price-earnings ratio	30	20	11
9	Market price	$ 64	$ 47	$ 29
10	Market price as % of			
	book value	333%	220%	122%

SUCCESS

In Table XXII, we show success. To be successful over the long run, the company must earn a high return on common book value to provide a strong long range growth rate in earnings per share. And this must be done with a capital structure which is not superficially jazzed up with high leverage. In Table XXII, we show return on common book value of 20%. If this is sustained, it should provide a high price-earnings ratio such as 40 times. In the five year period 1965 to 1969, IBM earned 18% on its common stock and had a price-earnings ratio of 39 times. With success, everybody wins. The original investors are millionaires many times over and the public stockholders, who bought in at $27, have increased their investment 8 times.

Table XXII

NOTHING VENTURED NOTHING GAINED COMPANY

SUCCESS

All Funds Generated in One Year Are Reinvested at the Beginning of the Next Year

Line		Year 7	Year 8	Year 9
1	Common equity			
	Number of shares			
	Total	300,000	300,000	300,000
2	Book value Per Share	$ 19.23	$ 22.12	$ 26.54
3	Total	$5,770,232	$6,635,767	$7,962,920
4	% Return on common			
	book value	15%	20%	20%
	Earnings for common equity			
5	Total	$ 865,535	$1,327,153	$1,592,584
6	Per Share	$ 2.89	$ 4.42	$ 5.31
7	Growth rate in earnings			
	per share	65%	53%	20%
8	Price-earnings ratio	40	40	40
9	Market price	$ 116	$ 177	$ 212
10	Market price as % of			
	book value	603%	800%	799%

ODDS OF SUCCESS

But what are the chances of such a success? The quotation above from the *Institutional Investor* makes the odds look very small. Management should appreciate that to be other than a flash in the pan ultimately requires a sustained return on common book value of 15% or more. What are the chances of achieving such a return for a new company? We cannot present reliable statistics because such statistics are hard to come by for companies of this type, many of which fail before they go public.

However, let's look at the Fortune Survey for the 500 largest companies. Only about one-fifth showed a return on equity above 15% in 1969 as follows:

Return on Equity	Number of Companies	Percent	
21.0% and above	26	5%	
19.0% to 20.9%	14	3	
17.0% to 18.9%	25	5	20%
15.0% to 16.9%	34	7	
Below 15.0%	401	80	
	500	100%	

Thus the number of large well established companies that earn 15% or more on equity are in the minority and some of the companies which are included in the group would not be there if they had sound capital structures.

Ventures into new fields, properly conceived, are highly desirable for society. And risk of failure is a natural part of such ventures. Unfortunately, new ventures, much like conglomerates, provide an opportunity for the promoter type of management to produce an impression of growth in earnings per share through unsound accounting and financing methods. Given the right atmosphere in the stock market, this leads to high price-earnings ratios which permit the promoters to take advantage of the gullible public and unload. The sharp run up in earnings per share is no indication of how a company will succeed in the long run. It will survive only if the company can produce products or services which can at least meet competition. And if it is to be a huge success it must achieve a major edge over its competitors, and continue to do so with new products coming from research and development. Then it will be able to achieve a sufficiently high return on common equity to sustain a high price-earnings ratio.

Now that we have finished our discussion about the right tool to use as a management guide for capital and financial decision making, we will back track and see in the next chapter what profits mean to stockholders.

WHAT PROFITS MEAN

TO STOCKHOLDERS

When management establishes a Profit Goal, it should understand its significance in terms of the long range return to its
stockholders. This includes an understanding of the relationship of a

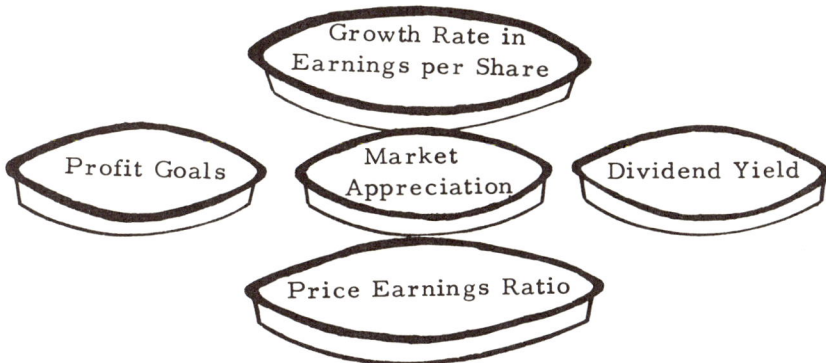

PIE IN THE SKY FOR STOCKHOLDERS.

Profit Goal to return to investors, price-earnings ratio, market price and market price divided by common book value.

While management should not attempt to control the market price, there will be occasions when management may wish to consider whether the stock is over or under priced. This question may arise if the company is contemplating the sale of new stock, if it wishes to repurchase its stock, or if it is going to use its stock for acquisition purposes. Also, some idea as to what its stock is worth may help management tell whether its investor relations program is getting across a complete story about its operations.

In this chapter we suggest a fundamental approach, consistent with the concepts of Cost-of-Capital, for management to take in trying to estimate the worth of its common stock. It is true that in the short run investors may vary in their preference for stocks in different companies or different industries. Each period in the stock market has its glamour stocks which are in vogue while stocks of other companies with fine basic performance may be ignored. The approach in this chapter will offer a frame of reference independent of short run market ups and downs. Our explanation will require a number of steps.

We start out by obtaining the return on common book value from a Profit Goal. As an example, we will use the figures for a minimum Profit Goal for a large conservatively capitalized industrial company as shown in Table XVII.

Long Term Capital	Amount	Rate	To Investor Rate
Debt	20%	6%	1.20%
Common equity	80	11	8.80
Total	100%		10.00%
Allowance Above Cost			2.00
Minimum Profit Goal			12.00%

We obtain the return on common book value as follows:

Return on Total Capital	12.00%
Less: Interest	1.20
Return Available for Common	10.80%
Common Book Value	80%
Return on Common Book Value =	$\dfrac{10.80\%}{80\%}$
=	$13\frac{1}{2}\%$

If the company has an established dividend policy, and there are no other factors that are expected to affect earnings for the common, then the growth rate in earnings per share from plow back can be determined readily. For example, if the company's dividend payout ratio was 50%, the compound growth rate in earnings per share, for a company with a return on common book value of 13½%, would be 6.75%.

RETURN RECEIVED BY INVESTORS

Now we have to consider briefly how stockholders receive their return. If the price-earnings ratio for a common stock remains constant, then the appreciation in market price will be the same as the increase in earnings per share. This is shown in Table XXIII, Part 1. Both earnings per share and market price increase at a 5% rate.

The investor also receives return from dividend yield. With a constant dividend payout and a constant price-earnings ratio, the dividend yield (dividends divided by market price) would be constant. This is shown in Table XXIII Part 2.

Combining the data in both parts of Table XXIII, investors receive a total return from the time they buy the stock until the time they sell as follows:

Annual growth rate in Earnings Per Share, producing a similar appreciation in market price with a constant price-earnings ratio	5.00%
Dividend yield	5.00
Total annual return to investors	10.00%

For a company which has constant figures for return on common book value, price-earnings ratio, and dividend payout ratio, the total return to investors is equal to the growth rate in earnings per share plus the dividend yield.[1]

---

[1] This statement can be shown to be sufficiently accurate, by discounted cash flow analysis, for the purpose for which it is intended.

Table XXIII

RETURN TO INVESTORS FROM MARKET APPRECIATION AND DIVIDEND YIELD

Part 1

RELATIONSHIP BETWEEN INCREASE IN EARNINGS PER SHARE AND MARKET APPRECIATION OF COMMON STOCK WITH CONSTANT PRICE-EARNINGS RATIO

Column	I	II	III	IV	V
Year	Earnings Per Share	Growth Rate in Earnings Per Share*	Price-Earnings Ratio	Market Price Common	Annual Appreciation in Market Price Common
0	$10.00		10	$100.00	
1	10.50	5%	”	105.00	5%
2	11.03	”	”	110.25	”
3	11.58	”	”	115.76	”
4	12.16	”	”	121.55	”
5	12.76	”	”	127.63	”

Part 2

YIELD FOR STOCK WITH CONSTANT DIVIDEND PAYOUT RATIO AND CONSTANT PRICE-EARNINGS RATIO

Column	I	II	III	IV	V	VI
Year	Earnings Per Share	Dividend Payout Ratio	Dividend	Price-Earnings Ratio	Market Price Common	Dividend Yield
0	$10.00	50%	$5.00	10	$100.00	5.00%
1	10.50	”	5.25	”	105.00	”
2	11.03	”	5.51	”	110.25	”
3	11.58	”	5.79	”	115.76	”
4	12.16	”	6.08	”	121.55	”
5	12.76	”	6.38	”	127.63	”

*A company earning 10% on common book value and paying out 50% in dividends would provide a 5% growth rate in earnings per share from plow back alone.

PRICE-EARNINGS RATIO AND MARKET PRICE
DIVIDED BY COMMON BOOK VALUE

Now let's use this idea for the company in our earlier example which has reached a constant return on common book value of 13½% on old and new investment, has a 50% dividend payout policy and, consequently, has a growth rate in earnings per share from plow back of 6.75%.

We have to assume a figure that will be acceptable to investors as a satisfactory return; in other words, we have to estimate the cost of common equity. What investors require in the long run as a reasonable return will depend on the risk of the stock as affected by such factors as the risk of the business, leverage, etc., and what returns can be obtained in alternative investments. Let's assume that investors would accept 11% as a minimum return from both market appreciation and dividend yield. Then by subtracting from 11% the growth rate of 6.75%, the dividend yield would have to be 4.25%. These figures can be summarized as follows:

Annual growth rate in earnings per share	6.75%
Dividend yield to make return to investors 11%	4.25
Total return acceptable to investors	11.00%

Now we can calculate the price-earnings ratio at which the stock would sell from the following formula, the derivation for which is shown in Table XXIV Part 1.

$$\text{Price-Earnings Ratio} = \frac{\text{Dividend Payout Ratio}}{\text{Dividend Yield}}$$

$$= \frac{50\%}{4.25\%}$$

$$= 11.8$$

Also, we can calculate the relationship of market price to common book value from the following formula, the derivation for which is shown in Table XXIV Part 2.

$$\text{Market Price Divided by Common Book Value} = \text{Return on Common Book Value} \times \text{Price-Earnings Ratio}$$

$$= 13\tfrac{1}{2}\% \times 11.8$$

$$= 159\%$$

We can summarize the relationship between return on common book value, return to investors, price-earnings ratio, and market price divided by common book value in Table XXV. In our example, the return to investors is 11% while the company earns 13½% on the common book value. This difference is due to the fact that the market price is above book value. If the return expected by investors is the same as the return on the common book value, the stock will sell at approximately book value,[2] provided the growth rate in earnings per share is due solely to plow back. This relationship will not hold if the growth rate in earnings per share is due to other factors, such as an increase in return on common book value.

Now let's look at an example in which the growth rate due to plow back, with a 50% dividend payout ratio, is supplemented by an increase in return on common book value and sale of stock above book value. We will assume that the return on common book value increases at a 2% annual compound growth rate from 10% to 12% in a ten year period. The average return on common book value during the ten year period would be 11%. We will also assume that the company sells two issues of common stock above book value, each of which increases earnings per share 0.5% or a total of 1%. This would amount to approximately 0.1% in growth rate per year over the ten year period. These figures are illustrated in Table XXVI. It shows a

---

[2]The return on common book value should be above Cost-of-Capital to produce a market price sufficiently above the true book value so that the company would receive net proceeds from sale of new stock which would be at least equivalent to the true common book value, after allowing for financing costs. For a company to be financially healthy and assure its ability to finance with common stock readily, it should earn a sufficient return so that its stock will sell at an additional premium.

Table XXIV

FORMULAS FOR DETERMINING PRICE-EARNINGS RATIO AND MARKET PRICE DIVIDED BY COMMON BOOK VALUE

Part 1

DETERMINATION OF PRICE-EARNINGS RATIO FROM DIVIDEND PAYOUT RATIO AND DIVIDEND YIELD

Since

$$\text{Dividend Payout Ratio} = \frac{\text{Dividends Per Share}}{\text{Earnings Per Share}}$$

$$\text{and Dividend Yield} = \frac{\text{Dividends Per Share}}{\text{Market Price}}$$

Then

$$\frac{\text{Dividend Payout Ratio}}{\text{Dividend Yield}} = \frac{\left(\dfrac{\text{Dividends Per Share}}{\text{Earnings Per Share}}\right)}{\left(\dfrac{\text{Dividends Per Share}}{\text{Market Price}}\right)}$$

$$= \frac{\text{Dividends Per Share}}{\text{Earnings Per Share}} \times \frac{\text{Market Price}}{\text{Dividends Per Share}}$$

$$= \frac{\text{Market Price}}{\text{Earnings Per Share}}$$

$$= \text{Price-Earnings Ratio}$$

Part 2

DETERMINATION OF MARKET PRICE DIVIDED BY COMMON BOOK VALUE FROM RETURN ON COMMON BOOK VALUE AND PRICE-EARNINGS RATIO

Since

$$\text{Return on Common Book Value} = \frac{\text{Earnings Per Share}}{\text{Common Book Value}}$$

$$\text{and Price-Earnings Ratio} = \frac{\text{Market Price}}{\text{Earnings Per Share}}$$

Then

$$\text{Return on Common Book Value} \times \text{Price-Earnings Ratio} = \frac{\text{Earnings Per Share}}{\text{Common Book Value}} \times \frac{\text{Market Price}}{\text{Earnings Per Share}}$$

$$= \frac{\text{Market Price}}{\text{Common Book Value}}$$

Table XXV

ILLUSTRATION OF RELATIONSHIP BETWEEN RETURN ON COMMON BOOK VALUE RETURN TO INVESTORS, PRICE-EARNINGS RATIO, AND MARKET PRICE DIVIDED BY COMMON BOOK VALUE

GROWTH RATE IN EARNINGS PER SHARE DUE TO PLOW BACK ONLY

Line

Growth rate in earnings per share from:
Plow back

Line		Return on Common Book Value		Earnings Retained (100%-50% Paid Out)		
1		13 1/2%	x	50%	=	6.75%
2	Increase in Rate of Return on Common Book Value					0.00
3	Other factors					0.00
4	Total growth rate in earnings per share					6.75%
5	Dividend yield to make return to investors 11%					4.25
6	Total return acceptable to investors					11.00%
7	Price-earnings ratio				=	$\dfrac{\text{Payout}}{\text{Yield}}$
8					=	$\dfrac{50\%}{4.25\%}$
9					=	11.8
10	Market price of stock divided by common book value				=	Return on Common Book Value x Price-Earnings Ratio
11					=	13 1/2% x 11.8
12					=	159%

growth rate in earnings per share of 7.6%. Assuming a total return acceptable to investors of 11%, the price-earnings ratio would be 14.7 and the market price of stock divided by common book value would be 162%.

However, note how this picture changes if the return on common book value stops increasing when it reaches 12% and no more common stock is sold. Then the growth rate in earnings per share would depend entirely on plow back and, with a 50% payout, would reduce to 6%. To provide investors with an 11% return, the dividend yield would have to be 5% and the price-earnings ratio 10 times.

Table XXVI

ILLUSTRATION OF RELATIONSHIP BETWEEN RETURN ON COMMON BOOK VALUE, RETURN TO INVESTORS, PRICE-EARNINGS RATIO, AND MARKET PRICE DIVIDED BY COMMON BOOK VALUE

GROWTH RATE IN EARNINGS PER SHARE FROM VARIOUS FACTORS

Line

Growth Rate in earnings per share from:

    Plow back

Line		Average Return on Common Book Value		Earnings Retained (100%-50% Paid Out)	
1		11%	x	50%	5.5%
2	Increase in Rate of Return on Common Book Value				2.0
3	Other factors—sale of common stock above book value				0.1
4	Total growth rate in earnings per share				7.6%
5	Dividend yield to make return to investors 11%				3.4
6	Total return acceptable to investors				11.0%
7	Price-earnings ratio			=	$\frac{\text{Payout}}{\text{Yield}}$
8				=	$\frac{50\%}{3.4\%}$
9				=	14.7
10	Market price of stock dividend by common book value			=	Return on Common Book Value x Price-Earnings Ratio
11				=	11% x 14.7
12				=	162%

DANGERS OF MISINTERPRETATION

We should explain that this approach should be used with great caution and understanding, otherwise, it could mislead management. As already stated, it assumes constant figures for return on common, price-earnings ratio, and dividend payout ratio. Furthermore, it does not differentiate between the return from dividends and market appreciation. As pointed out in our discussion of dividends in Appendix B, dividends are far more certain than the prospects of market appreciation. A lower overall return may be acceptable to investors if a substantial portion of it comes in the form of dividend yield.

This approach cannot be used at all for a company which pays no dividends. In such a situation, no matter what the price-earnings ratio, the return to investors from market appreciation alone would be equal to the growth rate in earnings per share provided the price-earnings ratio remained constant.

A serious drawback is the fact that the price-earnings ratio is overly sensitive when the price-earnings ratio is high and the dividend yield low. We can illustrate this problem by the following figures for a company which earns 13½% on its common book value with a 25% dividend payout policy.

Growth Rate in Earnings Per Share (13 1/2% x 75%)	10.125%
Dividend Yield to Make Return to Investors 11%	0.875
Total Annual Return Acceptable to Investors	11.000%
Price-Earnings Ratio	$= \dfrac{25\%}{0.875\%}$
	$= 29$

Now increase the growth rate to only 10.80% by dropping the payout ratio to 20% and the results would be as follows:

Growth Rate in earnings per share (13 1/2% x 80%)	10.80%
Dividend Yield to make return to investors 11%	0.20
Total annual return acceptable to investors	11.00%
Price-Earnings Ratio	$= \dfrac{20\%}{0.2\%}$
	$= 100$

This approach would suggest that the price-earnings ratio ought to increase from 29 times to 100 times.[3] It is clearly unrealistic.

The price-earnings ratio is also sensitive to assumptions made about the return required by investors. This is illustrated in the figures below.

Column	I	II
Return on common book value	13 1/2%	13 1/2%
Dividend payout ratio	50%	50%
Growth rate in earnings per share (13 1/2% x 50%)	6.75%	6.75%
Dividend yield	4.25	3.25
Total annual return acceptable to investors	11.00%	10.00%
Price-earnings ratio	$= \dfrac{50\%}{4.25\%}$	$\dfrac{50\%}{3.25\%}$
	= 11.8	15.4

Management's estimate about what the right price-earnings ratio ought to be goes up from 11.8 to 15.4 times if it assumes investors will accept a 10% return rather than 11%.

In view of all these reservations about the validity of this approach, you may ask whether it is worthwhile. Interpreted with understanding it can be helpful to management in viewing the connection between a company's basic earning ability and market price. For example, a company which reaches a level return of 12% on its common equity would be foolish to think in terms of a high price-earnings ratio in the long run.[4] On the other hand, a high return on common book value should not necessarily be assumed to produce a high price-earnings ratio. If the high return is accompanied by high risk due to the nature of the business or excessive leverage, then investors in the long run will require a higher return than such a figure as 11%.

---

[3]These figures appear to suggest that a company earning more that the Cost-of-Capital should have a low dividend payout. Dividend policy is not that simple. For a brief discussion of dividend policy see Appendix B.

[4]The common stock of such a company could sell at a high price-earnings ratio under some circumstances. For example, in a year of poor earnings, the price-earnings ratio in that year might be high in anticipation of improved earnings in the next year. Also, if such a company ran into a period of adverse earnings and then reversed the trend so that the return on the common book value increased in subsequent years it would produce a high growth rate in earnings per share and possibly a high price-earnings ratio, depending on how investors interpreted the growth rate.

DOW JONES INDUSTRIAL COMMON STOCK AVERAGE

Historically, these ideas have worked out for the stock in the Dow Jones Industrial Common Stock Average as shown in Tables XXVII Parts 1 and 2. Note that while the average return on common book value was 10.9%, the total return to investors was 9.1%. If the growth rate in earnings per share were due entirely to plow back, the stocks would have had to sell close to book value in order to return investors 9.1%. The fact is that they sold above book value, because the growth rate in earnings per share was due to other factors as well as plow back.

Suppose the figures represented by the Dow Jones Average were figures for an actual company. How might the company view them? The growth rate in earnings per share was 5.6% but 1.2% of this was due to two factors other than plow back. Let's assume the company decided that in the future it could earn as well as it did in the last five years. During that period the return on common book value was 12%, and the payout ratio 55%. This would produce a growth rate from plow back of 5.40%. Other factors such as sale of stock above book value might add 0.60% so that the growth rate in earnings per share would be 6.00% rather than 5.60% as in the past. Let's further assume that investors would accept a return of 11%. Then the figures would work out as follows:

	Return to Investors 11%
Growth Rate in Earnings Per Share from:	
Plow Back (12% x 45%)	= 5.40%
Other Factors	0.60
Total	6.00%
Dividend Yield Required	5.00%
Total Return to Investors	11.00%
Price-Earnings Ratio	$= \dfrac{\text{Payout}}{\text{Yield}}$
	$= \dfrac{55\%}{5.00\%}$
	= 11
Market Price of Stock Divided by Common Book Value	= Return on Common Book Value x Price-Earnings Ratio
	= 12% x 11
	= 132%

Table XXVII

DOW JONES INDUSTRIAL COMMON STOCK AVERAGE.*
RELATIONSHIP BETWEEN RETURN ON COMMON BOOK VALUE,
RETURN TO INVESTORS, PRICE-EARNINGS RATIO,
AND MARKET PRICE DIVIDED BY COMMON BOOK VALUE

Part I

10 YEAR AVERAGE 1960-1969

(Line References are to Table XXVII, Part 2)

Line

Growth rate in earnings per share from:

Plow back

Line	Return on beginning common book value †		Earnings retained (100% -60% paid out)		
1	10.9% (see line 9)	x	40% (see line 4)	=	4.4%
2	Increase in return on beginning common book value ‡				0.5 (see line 10)
3	Other factors (this is a balancing figure to equate the total to 5.6%)				0.7
4	Total growth rate in earnings per share				5.6% (see line 2)
5	Dividend yield				3.5 (see line 5)

---

*Includes the following stocks: Allied Chemical, Aluminum Co. of America, American Brands, American Can, American Telephone & Telegraph, Anaconda, Bethlehem Steel. Chrysler, DuPont, Eastman Kodak, General Electric, General Foods, General Motors, Goodyear, International Harvester, International Nickel, International Paper, Johns-Manville, Owens-Illinois, Proctor & Gamble, Sears Roebuck, Standard Oil of New Jersey, Standard Oil of California, Swift & Co., Texaco, Union Carbide, United Aircraft, U. S. Steel, Westinghouse Electric, Woolworth.

† The return on common book value is based on beginning book value because it is used to calculate the growth rate in earnings per share from plow back. The retained earnings came out of earnings during the year and are added to beginning book value to get book value at year end. Consequently, the compounding effect of plow back takes place during the year, with beginning book value as the base.

‡ The increase in return to the common stockholder from the increase in return on book value is only fully beneficial if there is no change in the leverage which would add risk to the earnings.

6	Total return to investors		9.1%
7	Price-earnings ratio	=	$\dfrac{\text{Payout}}{\text{Yield}}$
8		=	$\dfrac{60\%}{3.5\%}$
9		=	17 (see line 7)
10	Market price of stock divided by common book value	=	Return on common book value x price-earnings ratio
11		=	10.9% x 17
12		=	185% (see line 11)

Table XXVII

Part 2

DATA FOR DOW JONES INDUSTRIAL COMMON STOCK AVERAGE

Line		Average	1969	1968	1967	1966	1965	1964	1963	1962	1961	1960
1.	Earnings per share ($)		57.02	57.96	53.77	57.68	53.67	46.43	41.21	36.43	31.91	32.21
2.	Year to year growth rate in earnings per share (%)	5.6	(1.6)	7.8	(6.8)	7.5	15.6	12.7	13.1	14.2	(.9)	(6.1)
3.	Dividends per share ($)		33.90	31.34	30.19	31.89	28.61	31.24	23.41	23.30	22.71	21.36
4.	Payout ratio (%)	60	59	54	56	55	53	67	57	64	71	66
5.	Yield (%)	3.5	3.9	3.5	3.5	3.7	3.2	3.8	3.3	3.7	3.4	3.4
6.	Average high-low market price ($)		869	905	865	870	905	829	707	631	673	626
7.	Price-earnings ratio	17	15	16	16	15	17	18	17	17	21	19
8.	Beginning common book value per share ($)		521	477	476	453	417	426	401	386	370	339
9.	Return on beginning common book value (%)	10.9	10.9	12.2	11.3	12.7	12.9	10.9	10.3	9.4	8.6	9.5
10.	Year to year change in return on beginning common book value (%)	.5	(10.7)	8.0	(11.0)	(1.6)	18.3	5.8	9.6	9.3	(9.5)	(13.6)
11.	Market price—divided by beginning common book value (%)	185	167	190	182	192	217	195	176	163	182	185

On the basis of these figures, the company might justifiably expect a price-earnings ratio in the neighborhood of 11 times compared with the average in the last five years of 16 times. And the stock would sell around 132% of book value compared with 190% for the past five years. At 11 times 1969 earnings per share of $57.02 the stock would sell for $627.

However, circumstances can change, with both short and long term consequences for investors and for stock prices. For example, consider what might happen as a result of changes in return on book value over the next few years. The return in 1969 was below average at 10.9%, and might well be lower still in 1970—say 10%. Suppose it moved up to 11% in 1970 and back to its average level of 12% in 1972. The relevant figures would look like this:

	Beginning Common Book Value Per Share	Return on Common Book Value	Earnings Per Share Amount	Change	Dividend (55% Payout)	Retained Earnings
1969	$521	10.9%	$57		$31	$26
1970	547	10	55	(2.5)%	30	25
1971	571	11	63	15.0	35	28
1972	600	12	72	14.0	40	32

At the end of 1972, the stock still must sell at 11 times earnings if subsequent growth settles back to 6% and the investor is to receive an 11% future return from the sum of that 6% growth plus a 5% yield. This would result in a market price of $792, 132% of book value. But note two things that would have occurred. In the first place, earnings during the three years from 1969 through 1972 would have appreciated at a compound annual rate of 8% because of the improvement being experienced in rate of return. Therefore, investors would have received during that period, if the multiple held constant, a 13% annual return—8% in growth and 5% in yield. Secondly, the 1971 and 1972 year-to-year growth rates in earnings per share would have been inflated by the one-shot improvement in return. This might stimulate investors to be optimistic about the future and pay considerably more than a sustainable figure of eleven times earnings for the stock.

If the return on common book value did not increase for the years 1970 and 1971, as suggested above, but remained level or decreased, the market action would be the reverse of that outlined above.

Another factor which would affect the market price is the return that investors require. If interest rates stay high, investors may require a higher return from a common stock. That would decrease the market price. You can play around with these figures to see the effect of the various cross currents.

When we look at the historical results for particular company in terms of these parameters, there are various reasons why they may not tie together as we would expect:

1. The figures for return on common book value, price-earnings ratio and dividend payout ratio are not constant. And the use of average figures over a ten year period does not solve this problem.

2. The market price for a common stock is a result of what investors expected in terms of earnings per share rather that what actually occurred. Investors may get market prices out of line when their expectations are not realistic. Therefore, the total return investors received is not necessarily equivalent to common cost, because investors may have expected something quite different from what they received. As pointed out previously, only if we look at industry as a whole can we consider that the return to common stock investors may be approximately the same as common cost.

Such a broad index as the Dow Jones Industrial Common Stock Average, shown in Table XXVII, may iron out some of these factors, and therefore, the figures tie together fairly well.

We conclude this chapter by stating that we believe these concepts, properly interpreted, do provide a broad understanding of the relationship of profits to return on common book value, return to investors, price-earnings ratio, and market price divided by common book value. Therefore, we feel that it is a necessary link in understanding the chain of capital formation and decision making.

SIX

MANAGEMENT'S ATTITUDE TOWARD

EARNINGS PER SHARE AND MARKET PRICE

In spite of our insistence that management should not use current earnings per share for capital decision making, we have not hesitated to emphasize that management must be concerned with earnings per share because of the importance of this figure to the stockholders.

Earnings per share may have broader economic implications. The effect that earnings per share have on the market price of stocks, in turn, has an impact on our entire economy. Securities markets assist in the transfer of savings; they provide the investment liquidity which is essential to induce investors to advance capital. Investors would be much less inclined to buy securities if there was no easy way to sell them. Security prices affect a vast amount of the country's savings. And large swings in security prices affect the willingness of people to spend and the stability of our economy.

Obviously, there will be many mistakes made in evaluating security prices and also there will be much irrationality displayed in the market from time to time. Decisions on stock purchases have to be based on an appraisal of the future, which is difficult even in the simplest situations. Many investors do not have the skill to analyze securities so they make mistakes; others, impelled by the desire to make a killing, eagerly rely on rumors and hunches and get carried away with swings of speculative fever.

THE TRUTH

These distortions in security prices should not be magnified because companies give out inadequate information or misinformation and manipulate earnings. Publicly owned companies have an obligation to try to provide conditions under which it is possible for

121

investors to buy and sell their stocks in the market at fair prices. The prices of stocks are established on the basis of available information.

Each company should have an investor relations program for the purpose of providing all the necessary facts, both favorable and unfavorable, to permit the market place to arrive at a fair price for its stock.

ALL PERTINENT TRUTHS AND NOTHING BUT TRUTHS.

Management should do everything possible to report earnings so that they will correctly represent the company's earning power and so that they are easily understood. And in reporting to its stockholders, management should try to explain the causes of changes in earnings per share from period to period. An annual report should have one basic theme—what happened financially during the year, and why. Unfortunately, some annual reports glorify management's accomplishments, while hiding its failings. And some companies engage in financial reporting which ranges all the way from failing to report all unfavorable facts as well as the good, to puffing and yes, even deception—name it what you will.

Perhaps we need the same type of penalties applied to the reports, both written and verbal, issued by companies on their financial condition as now apply to material included in a prospectus for a new issue under the Securities Act. And it might not do any harm to make reports issued by brokerage firms subject to the same penalties. It just might have a very therapeutic effect and assist in evening out the flow of capital.

It is a sad commentary on some managements that the Accounting Principles Board of the American Institute of Certified Public Accountants is now having to tell companies to make earnings comparable when there are changes in accounting methods and estimates. But this is what the Board is apparently attempting to do in its proposed opinion dated February 16, 1970. The first paragraph is as follows:

> Changes in accounting principles and methods followed by a business enterprise may affect importantly the financial position and the net income of the enterprise, as well as trends shown in comparative financial statements. In view of the extensive use of comparative financial statements, including presentations of results of operations for at least two years and summaries of such results often for five or more years, it is important that changes in accounting be treated in a manner that will facilitate analysis and further the understanding of the companies.

Auditors should not have had to put the pressure on companies that have made pooling of interest acquisitions to restate comparative sales and earnings of prior years with the acquisition in order to show the correct earnings change.

Pooling of interests seemed to be much desired when a company bought another company above book value because this avoided reducing earnings by writing off the difference between the book value and the purchase price. However, purchase accounting seemed to be preferred when the shoe was on the other foot and the purchase was below book value so that the difference between book

124

EARNINGS PER SHARE AND MARKET PRICE

and the purchase price could be amortized and provided an increase in earnings.[1]

As we explained, when a high price-earnings ratio company buys a low price-earnings ratio company, there is a one time increase in earnings per share. It might be well to help stockholders understand this effect on earnings per share by explaining how much it amounted to in terms of the year's earnings per share. Heaven forbid such a thought! Don't explain—run out and buy another low price-earnings ratio company to get another one shot kick.

Some companies talk to analysts about their future growth rate in earnings per share. Have they really considered whether the rate can be maintained beyond a limited time? Have they determined how much is required from internal growth in earnings, how much from external growth? On the basis of their long range return on long term capital, what can their growth rate in earnings per share be with a sound debt ratio?

There is still much controversy over the reporting of earnings per share when a company has convertibles outstanding. Regardless of whether the methods being developed are the best that can be devised, thank goodness some effort is being made to focus the picture. With regard to convertible preferreds, it was interesting to hear one high flying financier comment that convertible preferred is just the same as common stock. It may be noted that one company with a large amount of convertible preferred had to announce that there were no earnings available for common stock after payment of the convertible preferred dividends. Try to explain to those common stockholders that convertible preferreds are just like common stock!

Fortunately, the break in the stock market in 1969 helped bring to light the weaknesses of some of the conglomerates. Prior thereto, when the conglomerate craze was in full swing, some of the business magazines did not use a very critical eye in reporting on merger minded companies, probably because they did not stop to evaluate the possible long range consequences—maybe they did not under-

---

[1] Opinion 16 of the Accounting Principles Board of the American Institute of Certified Public Accountants, issued in 1970, does not now permit a choice between pooling and purchase accounting.

stand. There were a few good articles[2] presenting the problem correctly, but investors were slow to heed them and some members of Wall Street preferred to ignore them and throw gasoline on the fire to keep things heated up.

As a result of acquisitions, the capital structures of some companies became a hodgepodge of complicated securities which defy analysis.

> **A company has just so much earnings to be divided between the various holders of long term securities. You can't make any more earnings by dividing them up in a complicated fashion, and in the long run the complications may make investors less interested.**

PRICE-EARNINGS RATIO TOO HIGH AS BAD AS TOO LOW

Some managements, in fact many managements, seem to judge their success in terms of the price-earnings ratio for their stock—the higher the better, whether justified or not. Typical of some of the statements coming from the high flying executives are:

> Everything has changed, the name of the game today is get the current earnings up, boost the price-earnings ratio in every way possible and use the inflated paper to boost current earnings again and again by more acquisitions.
>
> Look at the millions of dollars of stock value that such tactics create.

Just plain nonsense! No true values are created by such tactics. Isn't this a rather sad commentary on American management, if management's real job is to produce a fair return to investors on their investment? Management should not want its stock to be overpriced any more than it should want it to be underpriced. If it is overpriced a correction will have to take place in the future; some stockholders will have benefited, but only at the expense of others. This is merely

---

[2]See articles: "The Earnings Per Share Trap" by Marvin M. May, *Financial Analysts Journal,* May-June 1968. "Want to Get Rich Quick?" *Barron's National Business and Financial Weekly,* February 5, 1968. "Lost Charisma" *Barron's National Business and Financial Weekly,* September 1, 1969.

a redistribution of wealth rather than the creation of wealth. It is strictly a "Las Vegas" game with the stockbrokers skimming off commissions as the stock runs up and down.

If a stock appreciates in an appropriate relationship to earnings as the earnings grow, then the company will have a continuous group of satisfied stockholders who will be rewarded fairly for their contributions of capital. To promote this objective, management should not attempt to influence the price of its company's stock either by manipulating current earnings per share or spreading slanted financial information.

CONCLUSION

We conclude this brief book with this thought: Our free enterprise system needs statesmanship in financial management so that the true purpose of finance, which plays such a major part in our economy, will be achieved. The purpose of finance is to transfer, in an orderly fashion and without unnecessary complication, the savings of our nation from investors to corporations so that capital can assist in production. At the same time, investors should be rewarded fairly. Profits must be the carrot which indicates to management what to do. Profits must be thoroughly understood in terms of return on capital so that capital will be well managed. In this way, we help our free enterprise system achieve its goal to produce more goods and services at lower costs, thereby providing a higher standard of living for all.

TREATMENT OF RESERVES

IN CAPITAL STRUCTURE ANALYSIS

Reserve accounts are of various types. If a company takes accelerated depreciation for tax purposes but depreciates on its books on a straight line basis, a reserve for deferred taxes is created. This reserve represents a liability for taxes payable to the government in the future. It is not equity, but the liability will probably never be paid. The best way to look at this reserve would be as an interest-free loan from the government. In the event that the company's base of depreciable assets contracted or in the event of liquidation, this reserve would become in whole or in part a liability to be paid.

Should it then be included as long term debt? There is no uniformity of treatment by financial analysts. We prefer to leave such a reserve out of long term debt calculations and hence out of long term capital entirely, even though it can be viewed as an interest-free loan. The amount which can be "borrowed" in this fashion is not subject to normal credit considerations and does not affect the quality of a company's regular debt. Instead the amount of deferred taxes will be determined by a set of rules for the reporting of income to the Internal Revenue Service. A company will naturally want to maximize tax deferrals to the extent permitted by law and will derive an advantage from doing so. In no way will its debt capacity be reduced by the creation of tax deferrals. In fact, debt capacity may increase somewhat since this interest-free capital is available for investment in income producing assets and hence will improve the overall profitability of the company.

Reserves for investment tax credit are viewed in somewhat similar fashion, with all likelihood that they will never be paid, although for a different reason. They result from proration for book purposes of the investment tax credit over a number of years although it is applied to a single year for tax purposes.

In other cases, reserves may represent common equity. An example is any reserve for contingencies. Such a reserve is created by a charge on the income statement after paying taxes or as a transfer of surplus. It is a tax paid reserve and really nothing more than a sub-division of common equity capital.

A good example of a hybrid case is a bank reserve for loan losses. This reserve has several components:

1. An amount which will actually be required to offset loss inherent in the bank's present loan portfolio.
2. Deferred taxes arising as a result of special tax rules applicable to commercial banks which permit the establishment of such a reserve on a pre-tax basis.
3. A sub-division of common equity which would result after all losses applicable to loans were met and all taxes were paid. This part may be considered as common equity.

When a reserve has been created from a charge to the income statement which is deductible for tax purpose, a tax payment has been deferred. If the reserve had not been created more taxes would have been paid. Therefore, estimating the common equity value of a tax deductible reserve requires a deduction from the reserve of the amount of taxes that would have been paid if it had flowed through to common equity.

DIVIDEND POLICY

The purpose of dividend policy should be to maximize the return to investors from dividends and market appreciation over the long run by setting a policy which will attract the greatest stockholder interest. A company should adopt a policy which fits its economic characteristics and the type of investors who will be attracted to it. Loss of potential stockholder interest will occur if management attempts to set a dividend policy in order to attract a certain type of stockholder without regard to the nature of the business.

In considering the advantage of dividends versus retained earnings which will provide market appreciation through earnings growth, investors will place a different evaluation on each, depending on their individual desires. Cash dividends are certain, whereas there is a risk factor which must be attached to retained earnings because the company may not be able to use the capital successfully. For this reason cash dividends will ordinarily be valued higher than retained earnings. This would be particularly true of investors who want cash income. Some investors cannot legally buy a common stock which does not have a cash dividend record for a number of years. Cash dividends tend to help support the price of a stock as it declines and the dividend yield becomes attractive. On the other hand, some investors who are in a high tax bracket may want only appreciation.

As a guide for thinking, there are five basic cash dividend policies as shown below in terms of percentage payout. Brief comments indicate the types of companies which they might fit the best.

1. 0%   For a company with speculative characteristics which will only attract investors who are primarily seeking capital gains.

2. 5% Nominal   For a company in a transition period, from the type described in "1" to a more stable type of company, starting to pay dividends on a gradual basis in order to build a record.

3. 25% Low   For a high quality company which generates a high return

129

on capital such as 15%, providing a 11.25% growth rate in earnings per share from plow back. Such a company can do more for investors with a low payout because the high growth rate will produce a high price-earnings ratio.[1]

4. 50% Average   For a typical large industrial company earning 10% to 12% on the common book value, providing a 5% to 6% growth rate from plow back and a fairly generous dividend. Because of the variability of earnings of an industrial company a higher payout might make the dividend vulnerable to being cut.

5. 65% High   For a stable type of company like a utility which cannot earn a high return on its common book value but does have stability of earnings and therefore can offer a generous dividend without fear of cutting it.

In the final determination of dividend policy, refinements can be made for any one of these percentages. Of course, there are many more considerations in dividend policy than have been discussed here such as the importance of a pattern, the inadvisability of cutting a dividend and the principle that cash needs should not affect dividend policy for a financially strong company.

In conclusion, withholding dividends for the purpose of increasing earnings per share from plow back or to provide cash for expansion is not necessarily the right way to do the most for stockholders in terms of dividends and market appreciation in the long run. The appropriate dividend policy for a particular type of company must depend on all the circumstances surrounding the company.

---

[1] A common stock with high risk, due to the nature of the company's business or to excessive leverage, would not necessarily produce a high price-earnings ratio, because in the long run investors would require a high return.

CAPITAL STRUCTURE POLICY--

PROPER USE OF LEVERAGE[1]

There is a much debated question: How much leverage or senior securities should a company use in its capital structure? We cannot come to any conclusion about the proper debt ratio for a particular type of company in this short appendix, but we can give some of the thoughts that should be weighed in aiming at an answer.

Actually, any fool can go into debt to increase leverage and it can be done very quickly; it does not take any intelligence on the part of management. As long as a company's earnings are trending upward and there is a favorable stock market, leverage takes on a particularly attractive appearance. The financial analysts want earnings to advance as fast as possible and many of them advise companies strongly in favor of leverage.

However, a favorable period with good earnings is not the test of a company's financial policy. The test comes when a company runs into bad earnings and a stock market unreceptive to new equity capital. Such an adverse period cannot be foreseen by management because of the inability to forecast more than a limited number of years ahead with any degree of certainty. Then leverage, which looked so advantageous when earnings were good, may be the company's undoing. It is a very difficult, long and costly process to straighten out a company which has used debt excessively. In other words, capital structure is totally flexible as far as the relative ease with which debt can be added, but it is almost totally inflexible in terms of straightening out a company which has abused the use of debt.

Basically, there are three risks to which the securities of any business are subject: one, the risk of the business itself; two, a credibility gap risk when management makes stockholders suspicious because financial reporting is colored; and three, a financial risk resulting from unsound financial policies.

---

[1]For a discussion of Capital Structure see Chapter III1, *Long Term Financing,* by John F. Childs, Prentice Hall, Inc., 1961.

A company which uses debt excessively adds a financial risk for the following reasons:

1. It may be unable to raise capital at all.
2. It may be unable to raise capital without straining its credit.
3. It may have to cut its dividend.
4. It may have its capital costs increased by having to pay high rates and accept restrictive terms.
5. It may be forced into the common market when its stock price is depressed.
6. It may have a high price-earnings ratio while earnings are good, but a low price-earnings ratio with adversities—a yo-yo stock rather than one with a more consistent sound upward trend.
7. Although its earnings per share may be increased, if the risk to the common has been correspondingly increased there is no gain to the stockholders in the long run.

Debt does provide cheap capital and it should be used, but within reasonable bounds so that it does not add a substantial risk. The bounds depend on the risk of the business. Since the risk varies from industry to industry, this may mean an average debt ratio of 20% of long term capital for some industrial companies and, by contrast, 85% for some finance companies. And there will be variations among companies in an industry. *A company's ability to carry debt does not depend so much on the balance sheet relationship of the debt to long term capital as on the company's ability to earn and on the quality of these earnings. When we refer to a certain debt ratio as being satisfactory, we are assuming that the company is able to earn adequately.*

For financial planning purposes, a company should determine an average debt ratio target as well as a maximum. Use of the maximum should be reserved for times when stock market conditions and the outlook for earnings are poor.

You may run into the idea that in deciding on whether to finance with debt or common stock, you should compare the cost of debt with the cost of common on the following basis:

Interest cost of debt, after allowing for tax savings of interest, versus the earnings-price percentage for the common.

For example, assume that a company's stock sells at 20 times earnings, then the earnings-price percentage is 5%. In such a situation, it is sometimes contended that the common cost is 5% and that the company could raise capital on a cheaper cost basis if it could sell debt with an interest rate of less than 10%. Assuming a 50% tax rate, the net after tax cost of debt would be less than 5%.

There is nothing wrong with the figures, but there is much wrong with the comparison as a method for making a decision as to whether to use debt or common. Furthermore, the terminology is wrong as far as common stock is concerned because the earnings-price percentage is not the common cost;[2] the common cost is not based on the relationship of current earnings to market price but on investors' expectations of earnings. And statistical evidence points to the fact that the common cost has never been significantly below 10% for any type of company. It should be obvious that a company can always sell debt securities at a lower cost than the common cost, because debt comes before the common stock and the common stock must have a greater risk. With the greater risk, the common stockholders would expect a higher return than the debt investors. Therefore, the comparison is wrong as far as the cost of the two types of securities is concerned and it is an erroneous basis on which to make such a financial decision.

We conclude that increasing earnings per share by leverage is appropriate when senior securities are used in proper amounts. However, increasing earnings per share by the excessive use of senior securities is definitely not a policy which management can justify.

---

[2]It approximates the common cost only in the unusual situation wherein the company's current earnings are the same as investor's expectations of the company's future earnings. This is a situation in which investors expect no growth in earnings per share.

PURCHASE BY A COMPANY

OF ITS OWN COMMON

Company purchase of its own stock may represent an enticing way to increase earnings per share. But is it necessarily a good way? In order to answer this question we will discuss briefly the purpose and effect of repurchasing common stock. We will also say a few words about a reasonable price to pay for the common.

PURPOSE

A company may advance the following reasons for buying its own stock:

1. To provide shares for stock options.
2. To provide shares for acquisition purposes.
3. As an alternative to paying an extra dividend when a company has a large amount of cash for which it has no forseeable use.
4. To provide leverage for the common by sale of a senior security to obtain funds to purchase the stock.
5. To boost the price of the common.

What action a company takes with regard to this decision will depend on the price of the stock, the leveraged position of the company, the future needs for funds, etc.

Generally a poor purpose is to try to boost the market price because in management's judgment the stock is cheap. In the first place, it is difficult for management to tell whether its stock is over or under priced. Management has a tendency to feel that its stock is always under priced. Furthermore, such motivations border on market manipulation which management should assiduously avoid.

If there is excess cash available for which management sees no need in its expansion plans, it should consider whether there are other more appropriate uses than purchasing the company's stock. For example, if a company's long term debt is too high or there is too much preferred stock outstanding, these might be reduced to appropriate levels.

EFFECT

Besides the effect on earnings per share that results from a company purchasing its own stock, there is a decrease in common equity in relation to debt regardless of whether the purchase is from the proceeds of the sale of assets or from the sale of debt. Whether this is an important factor depends on the company's existing capital structure. The greater the market price of the stock above the book value per share, the greater will be the erosion of the common equity as a result of repurchases.

To illustrate how repurchase of stock erodes common book value, we will use the simple balance sheet shown in Table XXVIII. The common book value per share is $10. If the market price for the stock is $20 per share, and one share is purchased with the proceeds from the sale of the temporary investments, then the temporary investments would disappear from the balance sheet as well as $20 of common equity, even though the book value per share is only $10. After the transaction, the balance sheet would be as shown in Column II in Table XXVIII, Part 1. The debt ratio would increase from 17% to 20%. The common book value per share would be reduced from $10 to $8.89.

If the common stock were purchased by issuing debt rather than from temporary cash, the effect on the debt ratio would be much more pronounced. This can be seen from the two balance sheets shown in Table XXVIII, Part 2. The debt ratio would move up from 17% to 33%. The common book value per share would be reduced from $10 to $8.89.

PRICE

If a company's stock is over priced, it is a poor investment for the company as well as for investors. But how can management tell whether it is reasonably priced? If the price reflects expectations by investors of greater future earnings than management believes are possible, then the stock would be over priced and a poor investment. On the other hand, if the reverse is true and the price reflects expectations by investors of lower future earnings than management believes are possible, then the stock would be under priced. While these statements are sound in terms of the principles of Cost-of-Capital, they are probably not much help to management in making a decision as to whether or not the price is too high; investors' earnings expectations are hard to determine.

Management may consider the price in relation to past market performance and to future earnings as estimated by the management; the stock is then

Table XXVIII

RETIREMENT OF COMMON STOCK—EFFECT ON DEBT RATIO

Part 1

RETIREMENT WITH TEMPORARY INVESTMENTS

Line	Column	I Before Purchase of Common		II After Purchase 1 Share of Common at $20
	BALANCE SHEET			
	Assets			
1	Current Assets			
2	Temporary Investments	$ 20		$ 0
3	Other current assets	100		100
4	Total	$120		$150
5	Plant, net	50		50
6	Total assets	$170		$150
	Liabilities			
7	Current Liabilities	$ 50		$ 50
8	Long Term Debt			
9	Debt	$ 20 (17%)		$20 (20%)
10	Common equity (10 shares)	100	(9 shares)	80
11	Total	$120		$100
12	Total	$170		$150
13	Common Book Value per Share	$10.00		$8.89

Table XXVIII

RETIREMENT OF COMMON STOCK—EFFECT ON DEBT RATIO

Part 2

RETIREMENT BY ISSUING DEBT

Column		I	II
Line		Before Purchase of Common	After Purchase 1 Share of Common at $20
	BALANCE SHEET		
	Assets		
1	Current Assets	$100	$100
2	Plant, net	70	70
3	Total	$170	$170
	Liabilities		
4	Current Liabilities	$ 50	$ 50
5	Long Term Capital		
6	Debt	$ 20 (17%)	$20 (33%)
		New debt	20
7	Common equity (10 shares) 100	(9 shares)	80
8	Total	120	120
9	Total	$170	$170
10	Common Book Value per Share	$10.00	$8.89

looked at as an investment of the company's money, given management's knowledge of future prospects.

Management might use the approach suggested in Chapter Five.

One of the dangers in repurchasing common stock is the possibility of having to sell more stock at a lower price later on. Furthermore, reissuing treasury stock requires the filing of a registration statement.

In conclusion, we cannot give any definite answer regarding the advisability of a company increasing earnings per share by purchase of its own stock. Such a decision can only be made after a thorough review of all relevant considerations. We can, at least, say that this technique is not justified solely because it increases current earnings per share and because the stock is under priced.

INDEX

INDEX

C

D

E

F

R

S